75

Colorful Hexagons to Crochet

75

Colorful Hexagons to Crochet

The Ultimate Mix-and-Match Patterns
in Eye-Popping Colors

LEONIE MORGAN

St. Martin's Griffin
New York

75 Colorful Hexagons to Crochet
Copyright © 2015 Quarto Inc.
All rights reserved.
Printed in China.
For information, address St. Martin's Press,
175 Fifth Avenue, New York, N.Y. 10010.

www.stmartins.com

Library of Congress Cataloging-in-
Publication Data Available Upon Request

ISBN: 978-1-250-07434-8

St. Martin's Griffin books may be
purchased for educational, business,
or promotional use. For information
on bulk purchases, please contact the
Macmillan Corporate and Premium
Sales Department at 1-800-221-7945,
extension 5442, or write to
specialmarkets@macmillan.com.

First St. Martin's Press Edition:
January 2016

QUAR.CHEX

Conceived, designed, and produced by
Quarto Publishing plc
The Old Brewery
6 Blundell Street
London N7 9BH

Editor and designer: Michelle Pickering
Art director: Caroline Guest
Design assistant: Martina Calvio
Photographer: Simon Pask
Pattern checker: Therese Chynoweth
Chart illustrations: Kuo Kang Chen
Creative director: Moira Clinch
Publisher: Paul Carslake

Color separation by
PICA Digital Pte Ltd, Singapore
Printed in China by
1010 Printing International Ltd

10 9 8 7 6 5 4 3 2 1

Contents

Foreword

I love designing crochet patterns for people to use and enjoy. My craft room is a constant hive of activity, and Hubble the cat is always nearby to offer his opinion. The toppling piles of colorful skeins, the overfilled baskets of wool, and my trusty crochet hooks all wait eagerly to be used. I love gathering up yarns until my arms are full, arranging the woolly goodness into nice color combinations, and then, the best bit, designing a pattern. My hooks have been busy turning yarn into crochet hexagons—now yours can be, too!

Hexagons are as great as the traditional granny square and are as popular now as ever. Portable and versatile, you can take them with you when you are out and about, or whip up a hexagon or two in an evening. Before long you'll have a very satisfying pile of colorful hexes for your hexagon project.

I've filled this book with a selection of hexagons in a range of styles, plus five fabulous projects to crochet. You can mix and match hexagons to create a unique throw or blanket to treasure. Hexagons aren't used just for blankets, though; you can also make scarves, bags, pillows, and clothing. You can use the patterns and projects in this book as inspiration to create whatever you fancy.

Designing hexagons has been so much fun and I hope this book interests and inspires you to get your hooks busy crocheting gorgeous projects.

Happy Hooking!

Leonie Morgan

About This Book

This book is an eye-catching resource of multiple hexagons and projects for you to crochet. As well as the 75 designs, there is information on yarn requirements, crochet tools, and techniques.

Hexagon Selector, pages 8–11

All of the main hexagons are shown together here to help you compare and choose the right design for your project. The hexagons are organized by size, making it easy to mix and match the designs.

Tools and Techniques, pages 122–141

An illustrated, comprehensive, and concise guide provides everything you need to know to get started crocheting the hexagons.

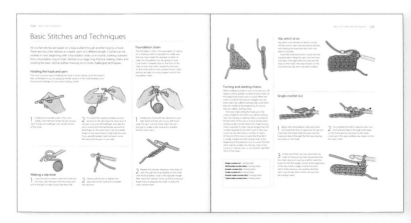

Hexagon Designs, pages 12–121

At the heart of this book are the 75 hexagons, many of which also feature color variations. Each design comes with a written pattern, chart, and clear photograph. Divided into beginner, intermediate, and advanced designs, you will also find one or two projects at the end of each section to give you ideas for how to use your hexagons.

The projects in this book specify the hook size and yarn weight used. All other hexagons were made with a size H (5 mm) hook and DK/light worsted yarn.

A key to the colors used in the pattern is included.

The name of the design.

Photographs show the end result of the main hexagon design plus any variations.

Skill level gives a rough guide to difficulty.

The size of the hexagon.

Instructions for special stitches used in the pattern are explained.

A written pattern takes you through the hexagon round by round or row by row.

Length estimates for each color provide a useful shopping guide.

Color variations include a photograph, color key, and written instructions (where necessary).

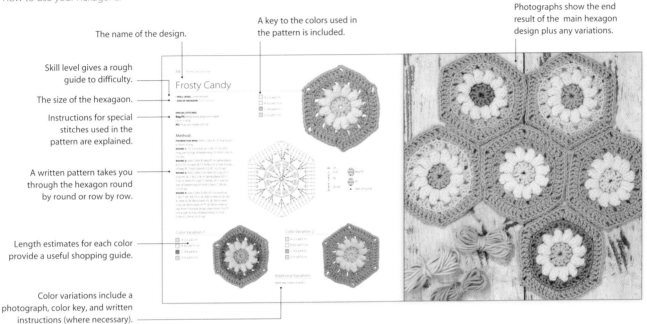

A full written pattern—including finishing instructions—explains how to make the photographed piece; or you could use all the information on these pages as inspiration for making your own version.

Alternating colors in the charts indicate each round/row.

A key to the symbols used in the chart is provided.

A diagram shows how to join the hexagons together to make the finished item.

The main photograph shows you how the hexagon can be used to make a beautiful project.

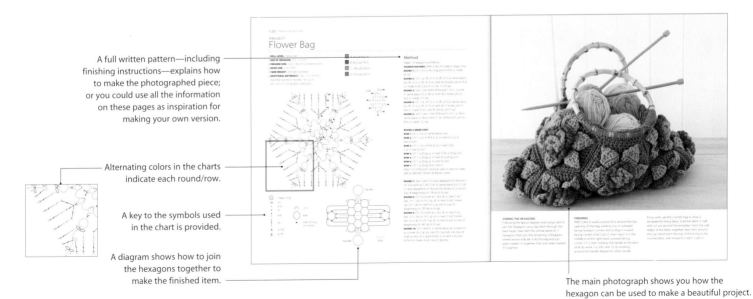

Hexagon Selector 7 IN. (18 CM) HEXAGONS

* page 12   * page 16   * page 18   * page 20   * page 22

* page 24   * page 28   * page 30   page 32   page 33

page 35   page 36   page 38   page 39   page 41

page 42   page 43   page 44   page 45   * page 50

* Hexagons marked with an asterisk also have color variations.

* page 52   * page 56   * page 58   * page 62   * page 66

* page 68   page 70   page 71   page 72   page 74

page 76   page 77   page 78   page 79   page 80

page 81   page 82   page 83   * page 84 (project)   * page 86 (project)

7 IN. (18 CM) HEXAGONS

* page 90

* page 92

* page 94

* page 96

* page 98

* page 100

* page 104

page 108

page 109

page 110

page 111

page 113

page 115

page 116

page 117

page 119

6 IN. (15 CM) HEXAGONS

* page 48 (project)

5 IN. (13 CM) HEXAGONS

* Hexagons marked with an asterisk also have color variations.

* page 14	* page 18	* page 26	page 34	page 37
page 40	* page 46 (project)	* page 54	* page 60	* page 64
page 73	page 75	* page 88	* page 92	* page 102
* page 106	page 112	page 114	page 118	page 120 (project)

Granny Hexagon

- **SKILL LEVEL:** Beginner
- **SIZE OF HEXAGON:** 7 in. (18 cm)

Method

FOUNDATION RING: With Color A, ch 5 and join to form a ring.

ROUND 1: Ch 3 (counts as 1 dc), 2 dc into ring, [ch 2, 3 dc into ring] 5 times, ch 2, join to top of beginning ch. End Color A. (18 sts, 6 ch sp)

ROUND 2: Join Color B in next ch-2 sp, ch 3 (counts as 1 dc), (2 dc, ch 2, 3 dc) in same place, ch 1, [(3 dc, ch 2, 3 dc, ch 1) in next ch-2 sp] 5 times, join to top of beginning ch. End Color B. (36 sts, 12 ch sp)

ROUND 3: Join Color C in next ch-2 sp, ch 3 (counts as 1 dc), (2 dc, ch 2, 3 dc) in same place, ch 1, [3 dc in next ch-1 sp, ch 1, (3 dc, ch 2, 3 dc) in next ch-2 sp, ch 1] 5 times, 3 dc in next ch-1 sp, ch 1, join to top of beginning ch. End Color C. (54 sts, 18 ch sp)

ROUND 4: Join Color D in next ch-2 sp, ch 3 (counts as 1 dc), (2 dc, ch 2, 3 dc) in same place, * ch 1, [3 dc in next ch-1 sp, ch 1] twice **, (3 dc, ch 2, 3 dc) in next ch-2 sp; rep from * 4 more times, then from * to ** once, join to top of beginning ch. End Color D. (72 sts, 24 ch sp)

ROUND 5: Join Color E in next ch-2 sp, ch 3 (counts as 1 dc), (2 dc, ch 2, 3 dc) in same place, * ch 1, [3 dc in next ch-1 sp, ch 1] 3 times **, (3 dc, ch 2, 3 dc) in next ch-2 sp; rep from * 4 more times, then from * to ** once, join to top of beginning ch. End Color E. (90 sts, 30 ch sp)

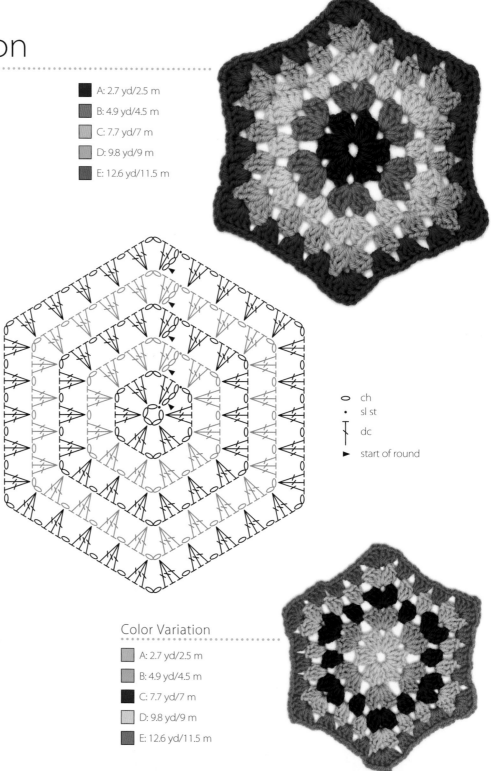

■	A: 2.7 yd/2.5 m
■	B: 4.9 yd/4.5 m
■	C: 7.7 yd/7 m
■	D: 9.8 yd/9 m
■	E: 12.6 yd/11.5 m

○   ch
•   sl st
†   dc
►   start of round

Color Variation

■	A: 2.7 yd/2.5 m
■	B: 4.9 yd/4.5 m
■	C: 7.7 yd/7 m
■	D: 9.8 yd/9 m
■	E: 12.6 yd/11.5 m

Lollipop

- **SKILL LEVEL:** Beginner
- **SIZE OF HEXAGON:** 5 in. (13 cm)

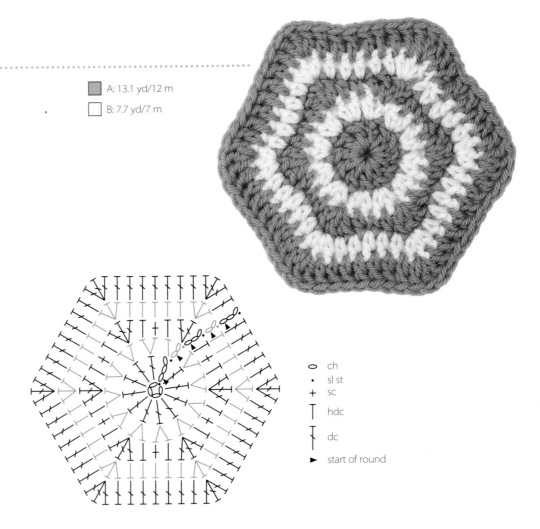

A: 13.1 yd/12 m
B: 7.7 yd/7 m

Method

FOUNDATION RING: With Color A, ch 4 and join to form a ring.

ROUND 1: Ch 3 (counts as 1 dc), 11 dc into ring, join to top of beginning ch. End Color A. (12 sts)

ROUND 2: Join Color B, ch 2 (counts as 1 hdc), hdc in same place, 2 hdc in next 11 sts, join to top of beginning ch. End Color B. (24 sts)

ROUND 3: Join Color A, ch 3 (counts as 1 dc), 2 dc in same place, [hdc in next st, sc in next st, hdc in next st, 3 dc in next st] 5 times, hdc in next st, sc in next st, hdc in next st, join to top of beginning ch. End Color A. (36 sts)

ROUND 4: Join Color B, ch 2 (counts as 1 hdc), [3 hdc in next st, hdc in next 5 sts] 5 times, 3 hdc in next st, hdc in next 4 sts, join to top of beginning ch. End Color B. (48 sts)

ROUND 5: Join Color A, ch 3 (counts as 1 dc), dc in next st, [3 dc in next st, dc in next 7 sts] 5 times, 3 dc in next st, dc in next 5 sts, join to top of beginning ch. End Color A. (60 sts)

○ ch
• sl st
+ sc
T hdc
T dc
► start of round

Color Variation 1

A: 13.1 yd/12 m
B: 7.7 yd/7 m

Color Variation 2

A: 13.1 yd/12 m
B: 7.7 yd/7 m

Salacia

- **SKILL LEVEL:** Beginner
- **SIZE OF HEXAGON:** 7 in. (18 cm)

Method

FOUNDATION RING: With Color A, make a magic ring.

ROUND 1: Ch 1, 6 sc into ring, join to first sc made. End Color A. (6 sts)

ROUND 2: Join Color B, ch 3 (counts as 1 dc), (tr, dc) in same place, [(dc, tr, dc) in next st] 5 times, join to top of beginning ch. End Color B. (18 sts)

ROUND 3: Join Color A in next tr, ch 1, (sc, hdc, sc) in same place, * sc in next 2 sts **, (sc, hdc, sc) in next tr; rep from 4 more times, then from * to ** once, join to first sc made. End Color A. (30 sts)

ROUND 4: Join Color C in next hdc, ch 1, (sc, hdc, sc) in same place, * sc in next 4 sts **, (sc, hdc, sc) in next hdc; rep from 4 more times, then from * to ** once, join to first sc made. End Color C. (42 sts)

ROUND 5: Join Color D in next hdc, ch 3 (counts as 1 dc), (tr, dc) in same place, * dc in next 6 sts **, (dc, tr, dc) in next hdc; rep from * 4 more times, then from * to ** once, join to top of beginning ch. End Color D. (54 sts)

ROUND 6: Join Color C in next tr, ch 1, (sc, hdc, sc) in same place, * sc in next 8 sts **, (sc, hdc, sc) in next tr; rep from 4 more times, then from * to ** once, join to first sc made. End Color C. (66 sts)

ROUND 7: Join Color A in next hdc, ch 1, (sc, hdc, sc) in same place, * sc in next 10 sts **, (sc, hdc, sc) in next hdc; rep from * 4 more times, then from * to ** once, join to first sc made. End Color A. (78 sts)

ROUND 8: Join Color B in next hdc, ch 3 (counts as 1 dc), (tr, dc) in same place, * dc in next 12 sts **, (dc, tr, dc) in next hdc; rep from * 4 more times, then from * to ** once, join to top of beginning ch. End Color B. (90 sts)

ROUND 9: Join Color C in next tr, ch 1, (sc, hdc, sc) in same place, * sc in next 14 sts **, (sc, hdc, sc) in next tr; rep from 4 more times, then from * to ** once, join to first sc made. End Color C. (102 sts)

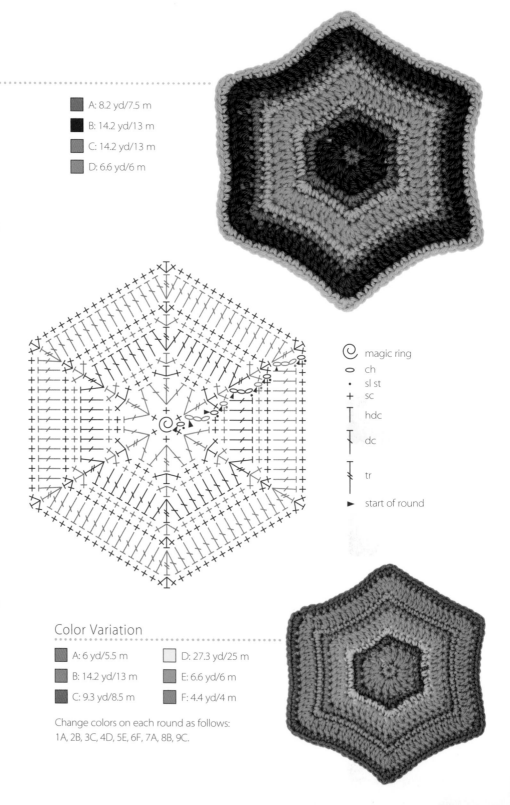

A: 8.2 yd/7.5 m
B: 14.2 yd/13 m
C: 14.2 yd/13 m
D: 6.6 yd/6 m

℮	magic ring
◯	ch
•	sl st
+	sc
T	hdc
╤	dc
⫽	tr
►	start of round

Color Variation

A: 6 yd/5.5 m
B: 14.2 yd/13 m
C: 9.3 yd/8.5 m
D: 27.3 yd/25 m
E: 6.6 yd/6 m
F: 4.4 yd/4 m

Change colors on each round as follows:
1A, 2B, 3C, 4D, 5E, 6F, 7A, 8B, 9C.

Fluro

- **SKILL LEVEL:** Beginner
- **SIZE OF HEXAGON:** 5 or 7 in. (13 or 18 cm)

Method

FOUNDATION RING: With Color A, ch 5 and join to form a ring.

ROUND 1: Ch 3 (counts as 1 dc), dc into ring, [ch 2, 2 dc into ring] 5 times, ch 2, join to top of beginning ch. End Color A. (12 sts, 6 ch sp)

ROUND 2: Join Color B in next ch-2 sp, ch 3 (counts as 1 dc), (dc, ch 2, 2 dc) in same place, [ch 1, (2 dc, ch 2, 2 dc) in next ch-2 sp] 5 times, ch 1, join to top of beginning ch. End Color B. (24 sts, 12 ch sp)

ROUND 3: Join Color C in next ch-2 sp, ch 3 (counts as 1 dc), (dc, ch 2, 2 dc) in same place, * dc in each st to ch-1 sp, ch 1, skip ch-1 sp, dc in each st to ch-2 sp **, (2 dc, ch 2, 2 dc) in ch-2 sp; rep from * 4 more times, then from * to ** once, join to top of beginning ch. End Color B. (48 sts, 12 ch sp)

TO MAKE 7 IN. (18 CM) HEXAGON

ROUND 4: Rep Round 3 using Color D.

ROUND 5: Rep Round 3 using Color E.

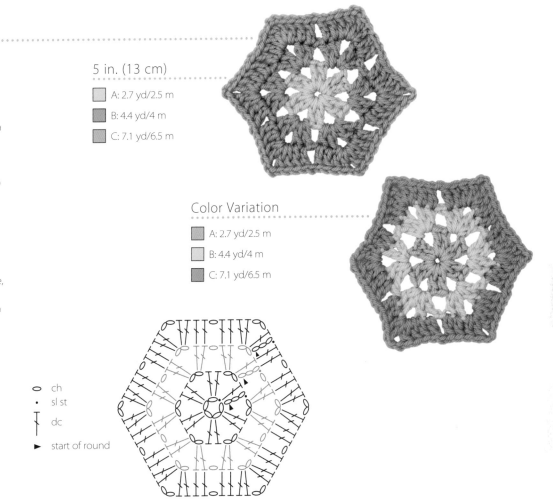

5 in. (13 cm)
- ☐ A: 2.7 yd/2.5 m
- ☐ B: 4.4 yd/4 m
- ☐ C: 7.1 yd/6.5 m

Color Variation
- ☐ A: 2.7 yd/2.5 m
- ☐ B: 4.4 yd/4 m
- ☐ C: 7.1 yd/6.5 m

○ ch
• sl st
† dc
► start of round

7 in. (18 cm)
- ☐ A: 2.7 yd/2.5 m
- ☐ B: 4.4 yd/4 m
- ☐ C: 7.1 yd/6.5 m
- ☐ D: 9.8 yd/9 m
- ☐ E: 12.6 yd/11.5 m

Color Variation
- ☐ A: 2.7 yd/2.5 m
- ☐ B: 4.4 yd/4 m
- ☐ C: 7.1 yd/6.5 m
- ☐ D: 9.8 yd/9 m
- ☐ E: 12.6 yd/11.5 m

Tiles

- **SKILL LEVEL:** Beginner
- **SIZE OF HEXAGON:** 7 in. (18 cm)

A: 1.6 yd/1.5 m
B: 3.8 yd/3.5 m
C: 5.5 yd/5 m
D: 7.7 yd/7 m
E: 8.7 yd/8 m
F: 9.8 yd/9 m

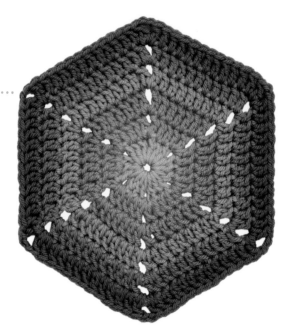

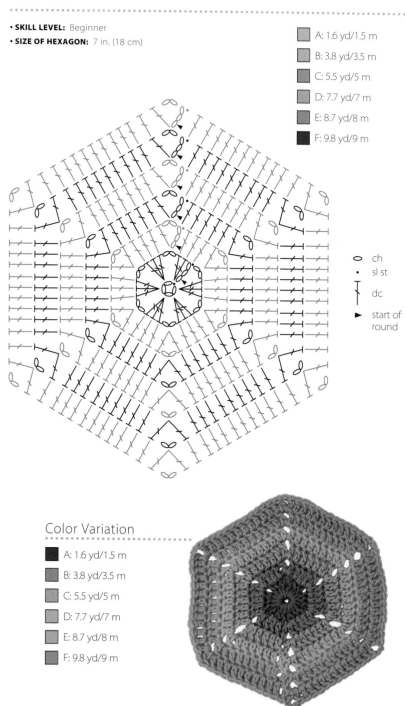

○ ch
• sl st
┼ dc
▶ start of round

Color Variation

A: 1.6 yd/1.5 m
B: 3.8 yd/3.5 m
C: 5.5 yd/5 m
D: 7.7 yd/7 m
E: 8.7 yd/8 m
F: 9.8 yd/9 m

Method

FOUNDATION RING: With Color A, ch 4 and join to form a ring.

ROUND 1: Ch 3 (counts as 1 dc), 2 dc into ring, [ch 2, 3 dc into ring] 5 times, ch 2, join to top of beginning ch. End Color A. (18 sts, 6 ch sp)

ROUND 2: Join Color B in ch-2 sp, ch 5 (counts as 1 dc, ch 2), dc in same place, [dc in next 3 sts, (dc, ch 2, dc) in ch-2 sp] 5 times, dc in next 3 sts, join to 3rd ch of beginning ch. End Color B. (30 sts, 6 ch sp)

ROUND 3: Join Color C in ch-2 sp, ch 5 (counts as 1 dc, ch 2), dc in same place, [dc in next 5 sts, (dc, ch 2, dc) in ch-2 sp] 5 times, dc in next 5 sts, join to 3rd ch of beginning ch. End Color C. (42 sts, 6 ch sp)

ROUND 4: Join Color D in ch-2 sp, ch 5 (counts as 1 dc, ch 2), dc in same place, [dc in next 7 sts, (dc, ch 2, dc) in ch-2 sp] 5 times, dc in next 7 sts, join to 3rd ch of beginning ch. End Color D. (54 sts, 6 ch sp)

ROUND 5: Join Color E in ch-2 sp, ch 5 (counts as 1 dc, ch 2), dc in same place, [dc in next 9 sts, (dc, ch 2, dc) in ch-2 sp] 5 times, dc in next 9 sts, join to 3rd ch of beginning ch. End Color E. (66 sts, 6 ch sp)

ROUND 6: Join Color F in ch-2 sp, ch 5 (counts as 1 dc, ch 2), dc in same place, [dc in next 11 sts, (dc, ch 2, dc) in ch-2 sp] 5 times, dc in next 11 sts, join to 3rd ch of beginning ch. End Color F. (78 sts, 6 ch sp)

Bracken

• **SKILL LEVEL:** Beginner
• **SIZE OF HEXAGON:** 7 in. (18 cm)

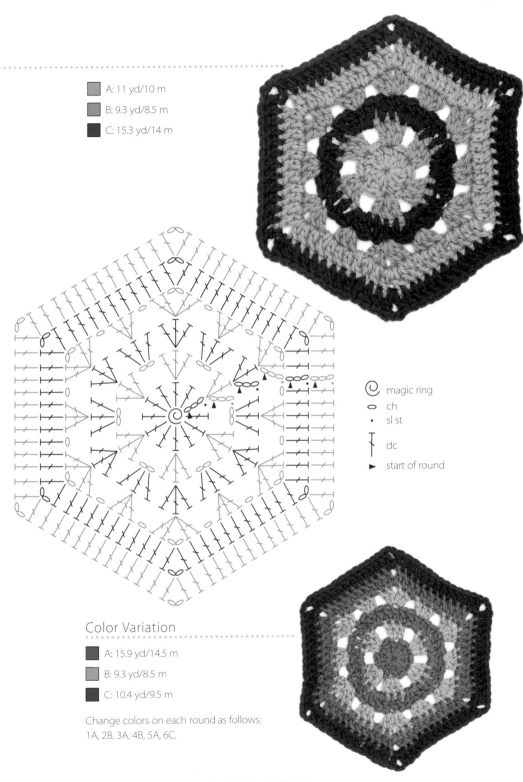

A: 11 yd/10 m
B: 9.3 yd/8.5 m
C: 15.3 yd/14 m

Method

FOUNDATION RING: With Color A, make a magic ring.

ROUND 1: Ch 3 (counts as 1 dc), 11 dc into ring, join to top of beginning ch. End Color A. (12 sts)

ROUND 2: Join Color B, ch 3 (counts as 1 dc), 2 dc in same place, [ch 2, skip 1 st, 3 dc in next st] 5 times, ch 2, join to top of beginning ch. End Color B. (18 sts, 6 ch sp)

ROUND 3: Join Color C in next st, ch 3 (counts as 1 dc), 2 dc in same place, [skip 1 st, 3 dc in next ch-2 sp, skip 1 st, 3 dc in next st] 5 times, skip 1 st, 3 dc in next ch-2 sp, join to top of beginning ch. End Color C. (36 sts)

ROUND 4: Join Color B in next st, ch 3 (counts as 1 dc), (dc, ch 2, 2 dc) in same place, * ch 1, skip 2 sts, 3 dc in next st, ch 1, skip 2 sts ** , (2 dc, ch 2, 2 dc) in next st; rep from * 4 more times, then from * to ** once, join to top of beginning ch. End Color B. (42 sts, 18 ch sp)

ROUND 5: Join Color A, ch 3 (counts as 1 dc), dc in next st, * (dc, ch 2, dc) in ch-2 sp ** , dc in each st and ch to next corner ch-2 sp; rep from * 4 more times, then from * to ** once, dc in next 7 sts and ch, join to top of beginning ch. End Color A. (66 sts, 6 ch sp)

ROUND 6: Join Color C, ch 3 (counts as 1 dc), [dc in each st to corner ch-2 sp, (dc, ch 2, dc) in corner ch-2 sp] 6 times, dc in next 8 sts, join to top of beginning ch. End Color C. (78 sts, 6 ch sp)

⟳ magic ring
◯ ch
• sl st
│ dc
▶ start of round

Color Variation

A: 15.9 yd/14.5 m
B: 9.3 yd/8.5 m
C: 10.4 yd/9.5 m

Change colors on each round as follows: 1A, 2B, 3A, 4B, 5A, 6C.

Lace Layers

- **SKILL LEVEL:** Beginner
- **SIZE OF HEXAGON:** 7 in. (18 cm)

□ A: 13.7 yd/12.5 m
■ B: 17.5 yd/16 m

Method

FOUNDATION RING: With Color A, make a magic ring.

ROUND 1: Ch 5 (counts as 1 tr, ch 1), [tr into ring, ch 1] 11 times, join to 4th ch of beginning ch. End Color A. (12 sts, 12 ch sp)

ROUND 2: Join Color B in ch-1 sp, ch 5 (counts as 1 dc, ch 2), dc in same place, * dc in next st, dc in next ch-1 sp, dc in next st **, (dc, ch 2, dc) in next ch-1 sp; rep from * 4 more times, then from * to ** once, join to 3rd ch of beginning ch. End Color B. (30 sts, 6 ch sp)

ROUND 3: Join Color A in ch-2 sp, ch 5 (counts as 1 dc, ch 2), dc in same place, * [ch 1, skip 1 st, dc in next st] twice, ch 1 **, (dc, ch 2, dc) in next ch-2 sp; rep from * 4 more times, then from * to ** once, join to 3rd ch of beginning ch. End Color A. (24 sts, 24 ch sp)

ROUND 4: Join Color B in ch-2 sp, ch 5 (counts as 1 dc, ch 2), dc in same place, * dc in each st and ch to next corner ch-2 sp **, (dc, ch 2, dc) in ch-2 sp; rep from * 4 more times, then from * to ** once, join to 3rd ch of beginning ch. End Color B. (54 sts, 6 ch sp)

ROUND 5: Join Color A in ch-2 sp, ch 5 (counts as 1 dc, ch 2), dc in same place, * [ch 1, skip 1 st, dc in next st] 4 times, ch 1 **, (dc, ch 2, dc) in corner ch-2 sp; rep from * 4 more times, then from * to ** once, join to 3rd ch of beginning ch. End Color A. (36 sts, 36 ch sp)

ROUND 6: Join Color B in ch-2 sp, ch 1, [(sc, hdc, sc) in ch-2 sp, sc in each st and ch-1 sp to next corner ch-2 sp] 6 times, join to first sc made. End Color B. (84 sts)

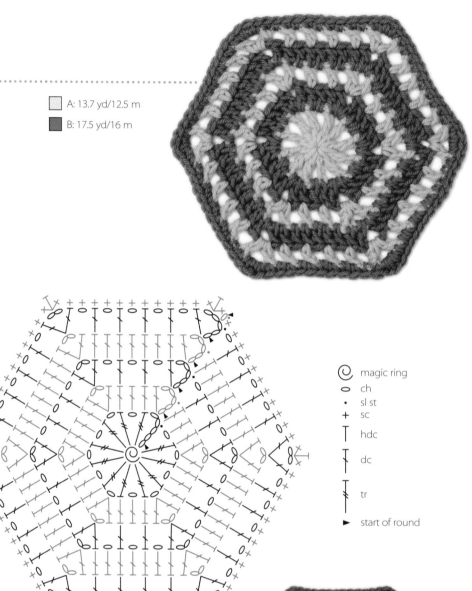

magic ring
ch
sl st
sc
hdc
dc
tr
▶ start of round

Color Variation

■ A: 13.7 yd/12.5 m
■ B: 17.5 yd/16 m

Lattice Wheel

- **SKILL LEVEL:** Beginner
- **SIZE OF HEXAGON:** 5 in. (13 cm)

A: 11 yd/10 m
B: 6.6 yd/6 m

Method

FOUNDATION RING: With Color A, ch 4 and join to form a ring.

ROUND 1: Ch 1, 12 sc into ring, join to first sc made. (12 sts)

ROUND 2: Ch 4 (counts as 1 dc, ch 1), [dc in next st, ch 1] 11 times, join to 3rd ch of beginning ch. (12 sts, 12 sp)

ROUND 3: Ch 4 (counts as 1 dc, ch 1), dc in same place, [ch 1, (dc, ch 1, dc) in next st] 11 times, ch 1, join to 3rd ch of beginning ch. (24 sts, 24 ch sp)

ROUND 4: Ch 5 (counts as 1 dc, ch 2), [dc in next st, ch 2] 23 times, join to 3rd ch of beginning ch. End Color A. (24 sts, 24 ch sp)

ROUND 5: Join Color B in next ch-2 sp, ch 3 (counts as 1 dc), (dc, ch 2, 2 dc) in same place, * 2 hdc in next ch-2 sp, 2 sc in next ch-2 sp, 2 hdc in next ch-2 sp **, (2 dc, ch 2, 2 dc) in next ch-2 sp; rep from * 4 more times, then from * to ** once, join to top of beginning ch. End Color B. (60 sts, 6 ch sp)

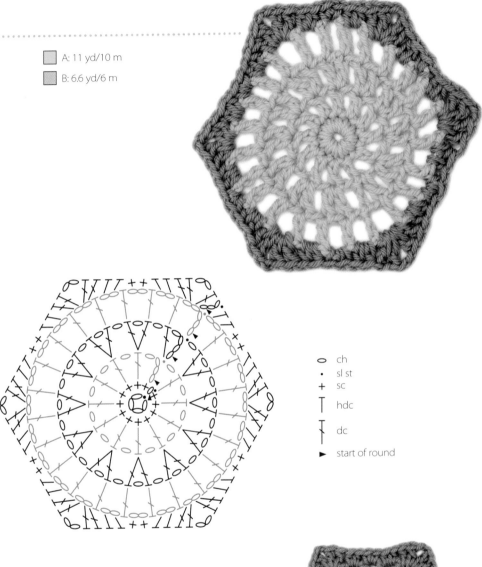

o	ch
•	sl st
+	sc
T	hdc
⊤	dc
▶	start of round

Color Variation

A: 11 yd/10 m
B: 6.6 yd/6 m

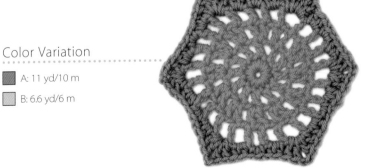

Mirror

- **SKILL LEVEL:** Beginner
- **SIZE OF HEXAGON:** 7 in. (18 cm)

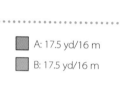

A: 17.5 yd/16 m

B: 17.5 yd/16 m

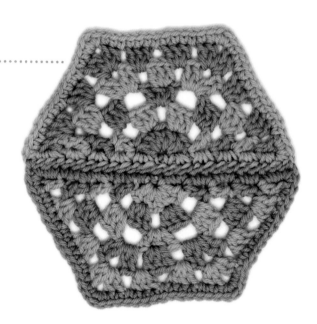

Method

FIRST HALF HEXAGON

FOUNDATION ROW: With Color A, ch 4 (counts as 1 foundation ch, 1 dc).

ROW 1: 6 dc in 4th ch from hook. End Color A. (7 sts)

ROW 2: Join Color B in first st of previous row, ch 3 (counts as 1 dc), dc in same place, [ch 2, skip 1 st, 3 dc in next st] twice, ch 2, skip 1 st, 2 dc in last st. End Color B. (10 sts, 3 ch sp)

ROW 3: Join Color A in first st of previous row, ch 3 (counts as 1 dc), dc in same place, [ch 2, 3 dc in ch-2 sp] 3 times, ch 2, 2 dc in last st. End Color A. (13 sts, 4 ch sp)

ROW 4: Join Color B in first st of previous row, ch 3 (counts as 1 dc), dc in same place, ch 1, 3 dc in ch-2 sp, ch 1, (2 dc, ch 2, 2 dc) in next ch-2 sp, ch 1, skip 1 st, 3 dc in next st, ch 1, (2 dc, ch 2, 2 dc) in next ch-2 sp, ch 1, 3 dc in next ch-2 sp, ch 1, 2 dc in last st. End Color B. (21 sts, 8 ch sp)

ROW 5: Join Color A in first st of previous row, ch 3 (counts as 1 dc), dc in same place, * [ch 1, 3 dc in next ch-1 sp] twice, ch 1 **, (2 dc, ch 2, 2 dc) in ch-2 sp; rep from * once, then from * to ** once, 2 dc in last st. End Color A. (30 sts, 11 ch sp)

ROUND 6: Join Color B in first st of previous row, ch 1, (sc, hdc, sc) in same place, [sc in each st and ch-1 sp to next corner ch-2 sp, (sc, hdc, sc) in corner ch-2 sp] twice, sc in each st and ch-1 sp to last st of previous row, (sc, hdc, sc) in last st, along bottom edge work 2 sc into side of each st, 1 sc into foundation ch, 2 sc into side of each st, join to first sc made. End Color A. (70 sts)

SECOND HALF HEXAGON

Repeat instructions above, alternating Colors A and B, to make second half hexagon. Sew the two half hexagons together using an overcast seam.

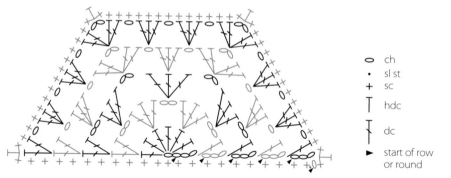

○	ch
•	sl st
+	sc
⊤	hdc
⊤	dc
►	start of row or round

Color Variation

A: 17.5 yd/16 m

B: 17.5 yd/16 m

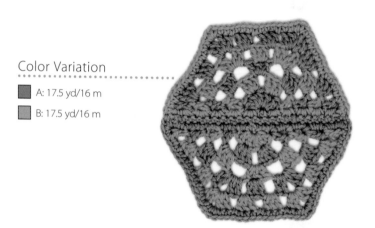

Fiesta

- **SKILL LEVEL:** Beginner
- **SIZE OF HEXAGON:** 7 in. (18 cm)

Method

FOUNDATION RING: With Color A, ch 4 and join to form a ring.

ROUND 1: Ch 3 (counts as 1 dc), 11 dc into ring, join to top of beginning ch. End Color A. (12 sts)

ROUND 2: Join Color B, ch 2 (counts as 1 hdc), hdc in same place, 2 hdc in next 11 sts, join to top of beginning ch. End Color B. (24 sts)

ROUND 3: Join Color C, ch 1, (sc, ch 2, sc) in same place, * sc in next 3 sts **, (sc, ch 2, sc) in next st; rep from * 4 more times, then from * to ** once, join to first sc made. End Color C. (30 sts, 6 ch sp)

ROUND 4: Join Color D in ch-2 sp, ch 3 (counts as 1 dc), 2 dc in same place, * dc in next 5 sts **, 3 dc in ch-2 sp; rep from * 4 more times, then from * to ** once, join to top of beginning ch. End Color D. (48 sts)

ROUND 5: Join Color E, ch 2 (counts as 1 hdc), * (hdc, ch 2, hdc) in next st **, hdc in next 7 sts; rep from * 4 more times, then from * to ** once, hdc in next 6 sts, join to top of beginning ch. End Color E. (54 sts, 6 ch sp)

ROUND 6: Join Color F in ch-2 sp, ch 1, (sc, ch 2, sc) in same place, * sc in next 9 sts **, (sc, ch 2, sc) in next ch-2 sp; rep from * 4 more times, then from * to ** once, join to first sc made. End Color F. (66 sts, 6 ch sp)

ROUND 7: Join Color G in ch-2 sp, ch 3 (counts as 1 dc), 2 dc in same place, [dc in each st to next ch-2 sp, 3 dc in ch-2 sp] 5 times, dc in next 11 sts, join to top of beginning ch. End Color G. (84 sts)

ROUND 8: Join Color H, ch 2 (counts as 1 hdc), * (2 hdc, 1 dc, 2 hdc) in next st **, hdc in next 13 sts; rep from * 4 more times, then from * to ** once, hdc in next 12 sts, join to top of beginning ch. End Color H. (108 sts)

A: 2.2 yd/2 m
B: 2.7 yd/2.5 m
C: 2.7 yd/2.5 m
D: 6.6 yd/6 m
E: 6 yd/5.5 m
F: 4.9 yd/4.5 m
G: 11 yd/10 m
H: 10.4 yd/9.5 m

o ch
• sl st
+ sc
T hdc
⊤ dc
► start of round

Color Variation

A: 2.2 yd/2 m
B: 2.7 yd/2.5 m
C: 2.7 yd/2.5 m
D: 6.6 yd/6 m
E: 6 yd/5.5 m
F: 4.9 yd/4.5 m
G: 11 yd/10 m
H: 10.4 yd/9.5 m

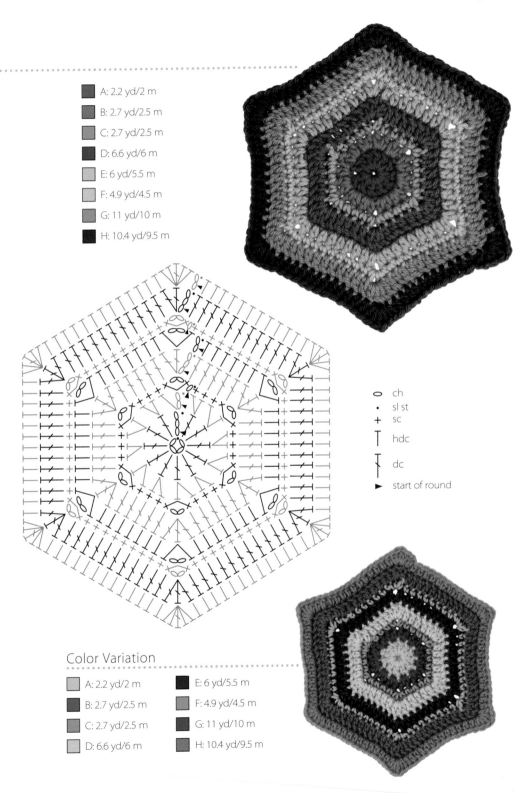

Marrakesh

- **SKILL LEVEL:** Beginner
- **SIZE OF HEXAGON:** 7 in. (18 cm)

Method

FOUNDATION RING: With Color A, ch 4 and join to form a ring.

ROUND 1: Ch 2 (counts as 1 hdc), 11 hdc into ring, join to top of beginning ch. End Color A. (12 sts)

ROUND 2: Join Color B, ch 2 (counts as 1 hdc), [3 hdc in next st, hdc in next st] 5 times, 3 hdc in next st, join to top of beginning ch. End Color B. (24 sts)

ROUND 3: Join Color C, ch 2 (counts as 1 hdc), hdc in next st, [3 hdc in next st, hdc in next 3 sts] 5 times, 3 hdc in next st, hdc in next st, join to top of beginning ch. End Color C. (36 sts)

ROUND 4: Join Color D, ch 2 (counts as 1 hdc), hdc in next 2 sts, [3 hdc in next st, hdc in next 5 sts] 5 times, 3 hdc in next st, hdc in next 2 sts, join to top of beginning ch. End Color D. (48 sts)

ROUND 5: Join Color E, ch 2 (counts as 1 hdc), hdc in next 3 sts, [3 hdc in next st, hdc in next 7 sts] 5 times, 3 hdc in next st, hdc in next 3 sts, join to top of beginning ch. End Color E. (60 sts)

ROUND 6: Join Color F, ch 2 (counts as 1 hdc), hdc in next 4 sts, [3 hdc in next st, hdc in next 9 sts] 5 times, 3 hdc in next st, hdc in next 4 sts, join to top of beginning ch. End Color F. (72 sts)

ROUND 7: Join Color A, ch 2 (counts as 1 hdc), hdc in next 5 sts, [3 hdc in next st, hdc in next 11 sts] 5 times, 3 hdc in next st, hdc in next 5 sts, join to top of beginning ch. End Color A. (84 sts)

ROUND 8: Join Color C, ch 2 (counts as 1 hdc), hdc in next 6 sts, [3 hdc in next st, hdc in next 13 sts] 5 times, 3 hdc in next st, hdc in next 6 sts, join to top of beginning ch. End Color C. (96 sts)

A: 9.8 yd/9 m

B: 2.2 yd/2 m

C: 13.1 yd/12 m

D: 4.4 yd/4 m

E: 6 yd/5.5 m

F: 7.1 yd/6.5 m

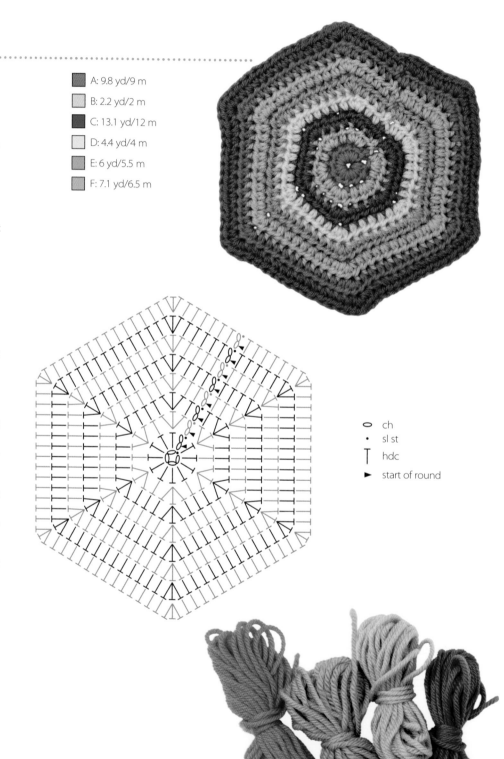

○ ch

• sl st

T hdc

► start of round

Zahra

- **SKILL LEVEL:** Beginner
- **SIZE OF HEXAGON:** 7 in. (18 cm)

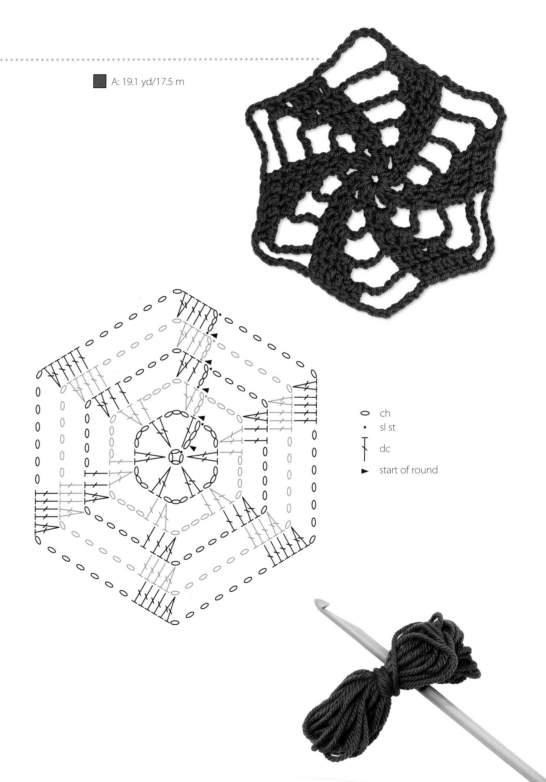

■ A: 19.1 yd/17.5 m

Method

FOUNDATION RING: With Color A, ch 4 and join to form a ring.

ROUND 1: Ch 3 (counts as 1 dc), dc into ring, [ch 3, 2 dc into ring] 5 times, ch 3, join to top of beginning ch. (12 sts, 6 ch sp)

ROUND 2: Sl st into next st, ch 3 (counts as 1 dc), * 2 dc in ch-3 sp, ch 4, skip 1 st **, dc in next st; rep from * 4 more times, then from * to ** once, join to top of beginning ch. (18 sts, 6 ch sp)

ROUND 3: Sl st into next st, ch 3 (counts as 1 dc), dc in next st, * 2 dc in ch-4 sp, ch 5, skip 1 st **, dc in next 2 sts; rep from * 4 more times, then from * to ** once, join to top of beginning ch. (24 sts, 6 ch sp)

ROUND 4: Sl st into next st, ch 3 (counts as 1 dc), dc in next 2 sts, * 2 dc in ch-5 sp, ch 6, skip 1 st **, dc in next 3 sts; rep from * 4 more times, then from * to ** once, join to top of beginning ch. (30 sts, 6 ch sp)

ROUND 5: Sl st into next st, ch 3 (counts as 1 dc), dc in next 3 sts, * 2 dc in ch-6 sp, ch 7, skip 1 st **, dc in next 4 sts; rep from * 4 more times, then from * to ** once, join to top of beginning ch. End Color A. (36 sts, 6 ch sp)

○ ch
• sl st
⊤ dc
▶ start of round

Runde

- **SKILL LEVEL:** Beginner
- **SIZE OF HEXAGON:** 5 in. (13 cm)

Method

FOUNDATION RING: With Color A, ch 4 and join to form a ring.

ROUND 1: Ch 2 (counts as 1 hdc), 11 hdc into ring, join to top of beginning ch. End Color A. (12 sts)

ROUND 2: Join Color B, ch 1 and sc in same place, [ch 3, skip 1 st, sc in next st] 5 times, ch 3, join to first sc made. End Color B. (6 sts, 6 ch sp)

ROUND 3: Join Color C in next ch-3 sp, ch 3 (counts as 1 dc), 2 dc in same place, [ch 1, 3 dc in next ch-3 sp] 5 times, ch 1, join to top of beginning ch. End Color C. (18 sts, 6 ch sp)

ROUND 4: Join Color B in previous ch-1 sp, ch 1 and sc in same place, [ch 4, skip 3 sts, sc in next ch-1 sp] 5 times, ch 4, skip 3 sts, join to first sc made. End Color B. (6 sts, 6 ch sp)

ROUND 5: Join Color D in next ch-4 sp, ch 3 (counts as 1 dc), (2 dc, ch 2, 3 dc) in same place, [ch 1, skip 1 st, (3 dc, ch 2, 3 dc) in next ch-4 sp] 5 times, ch 1, join to top of beginning ch. End Color D. (36 sts, 12 ch sp)

ROUND 6: Join Color B in next ch-2 sp, ch 1, [(sc, ch 3, sc) in ch-2 sp, ch 3, skip 3 sts, sc in ch-1 sp, ch 3, skip 3 sts] 6 times, join to first sc made. End Color B. (18 sts, 18 ch sp)

ROUND 7: Join Color E in next ch-3 sp, ch 3 (counts as 1 dc), (dc, ch 2, 2 dc) in same place, * [ch 1, skip 1 st, 3 dc in next ch-3 sp] twice, ch 1, skip 1 st **, (2 dc, ch 2, 2 dc) in next ch-3 sp; rep from * 4 more times, then from * to ** once, join to top of beginning ch. End Color E. (60 sts, 24 ch sp)

A: 1.6 yd/1.5 m
B: 6 yd/5.5 m
C: 2.7 yd/2.5 m
D: 5.5 yd/5 m
E: 8.2 yd/7.5 m

○ ch
• sl st
+ sc
T hdc
╪ dc
▶ start of round

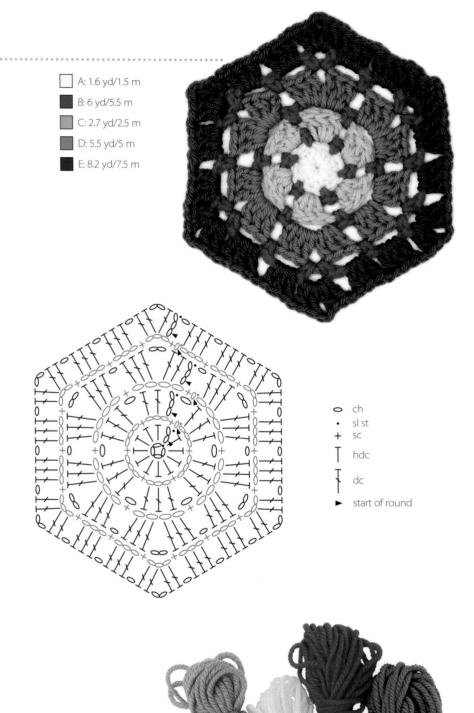

Alesund

- **SKILL LEVEL:** Beginner
- **SIZE OF HEXAGON:** 7 in. (18 cm)

Method

FOUNDATION RING: With Color A, ch 4 and join to form a ring.

ROUND 1: Ch 3 (counts as 1 dc), 2 dc into ring, [ch 2, 3 dc into ring] 5 times, ch 2, join to top of beginning ch. End Color A. (18 sts, 6 ch sp)

ROUND 2: Join Color B in next ch-2 sp, ch 1, [(sc, ch 2, sc) in ch-2 sp, ch 3, skip 3 sts] 6 times, join to first sc made. End Color B. (12 sts, 12 ch sp)

ROUND 3: Join Color C in next ch-2 sp, ch 3 (counts as 1 dc), (2 dc, ch 2, 3 dc) in same place, [ch 1, skip 1 st, 3 dc in ch-3 sp, ch 1, skip 1 st, (3 dc, ch 2, 3 dc) in next ch-2 sp] 5 times, ch 1, skip 1 st, 3 dc in ch-3 sp, ch 1, skip 1 st, join to top of beginning ch. End Color C. (54 sts, 18 ch sp)

ROUND 4: Join Color B in next ch-2 sp, ch 1, [(sc, ch 2, sc) in ch-2 sp, [ch 3, skip 3 sts, sc in ch-1 sp] twice, ch 3, skip 3 sts] 6 times, join to first sc made. End Color B. (24 sts, 24 ch sp)

ROUND 5: Join Color D in next ch-2 sp, ch 3 (counts as 1 dc), (2 dc, ch 2, 3 dc) in same place, * [ch 1, skip 1 st, 3 dc in next ch-3 sp] 3 times, ch 1 **, (3 dc, ch 2, 3 dc) in next ch-2 sp; rep from * 4 mores times, then from * to ** once, join to top of beginning ch. End Color D. (120 sts, 30 ch sp)

ROUND 6: Join Color B in next ch-2 sp, ch 1, [(sc, ch 2, sc) in ch-2 sp, (ch 3, skip 3 sts, sc in ch-1 sp) 4 times, ch 3] 6 times, join to first sc made. End Color B. (36 sts, 36 ch sp)

A: 2.7 yd/2.5 m
B: 11.5 yd/10.5 m
C: 7.7 yd/7 m
D: 12.6 yd/11.5 m

○   ch
•   sl st
+   sc
†   dc
►   start of round

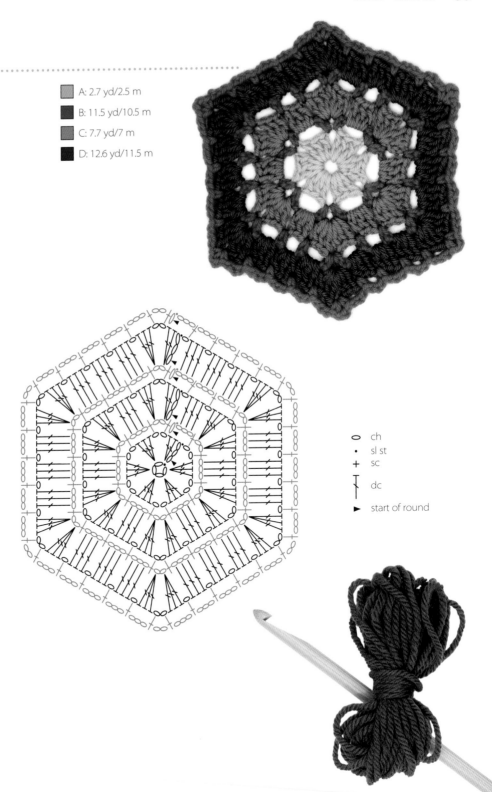

Spring Stripes

- **SKILL LEVEL:** Beginner
- **SIZE OF HEXAGON:** 7 in. (18 cm)

A: 9.8 yd/9 m
B: 5.5 yd/5 m
C: 6.6 yd/6 m
D: 7.7 yd/7 m
E: 8.2 yd/7.5 m
F: 8.7 yd/8 m

Method

FOUNDATION ROW: With Color A, ch 15.

ROW 1: 2 sc in 2nd ch from hook, sc in next 12 ch, 2 sc in last ch, turn. (16 sts)

ROW 2: Ch 1, sc in each st to end, turn. End Color A.

ROW 3: Join Color B, ch 1, 2 sc in first st, sc in each st to last, 2 sc in last st, turn. (18 sts)

ROW 4: Ch 1, sc in each st to end, turn. End Color B.

ROW 5: Join Color C, ch 1, 2 sc in first st, sc in each st to last, 2 sc in last st, turn. (20 sts)

ROW 6: Ch 1, sc in each st to end, turn. End Color C.

ROWS 7–8: Repeat Rows 5–6 using Color D. (22 sts)

ROWS 9–10: Repeat Rows 5–6 using Color E. (24 sts)

ROWS 11–12: Repeat Rows 5–6 using Color F. (26 sts)

ROW 13: Repeat Row 5 using Color A. (28 sts)

ROW 14: Ch 1, sc2tog, sc in each st to last 2 sts, sc2tog, turn. End Color A. (26 sts)

ROW 15: Join Color F, ch 1, sc in each st to end, turn.

ROW 16: Ch 1, sc2tog, sc in each st to last 2 sts, sc2tog, turn. End Color F. (24 sts)

ROWS 17–18: Repeat Rows 15–16 using Color E. (22 sts)

ROWS 19–20: Repeat Rows 15–16 using Color D. (20 sts)

ROWS 21–22: Repeat Rows 15–16 using Color C. (18 sts)

ROWS 23–24: Repeat Rows 15–16 using Color B. (16 sts)

ROWS 25–26: Repeat Rows 15–16 using Color A. (14 sts)

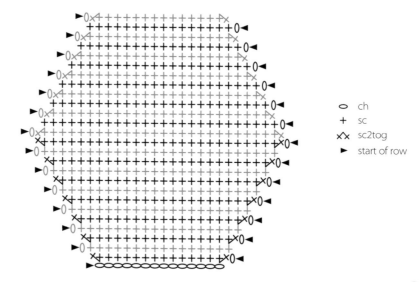

○ ch
+ sc
✕✕ sc2tog
► start of row

Springtime

- **SKILL LEVEL:** Beginner
- **SIZE OF HEXAGON:** 5 in. (13 cm)

Method

FOUNDATION RING: With Color A, ch 4 and join to form a ring.

ROUND 1: Ch 1, 12 sc into ring, join to first sc made. End Color A. (12 sts)

ROUND 2: Join Color B, ch 1, 2 sc in next st, [sc in next st, 2 sc in next st] 5 times, sc in next st, join to first sc made. End Color B. (18 sts)

ROUND 3: Join Color C, ch 1, [2 sc in next 2 sts, sc in next st] 6 times, join to first sc made. End Color C. (30 sts)

ROUND 4: Join Color D, ch 1 and sc in same place, [2 sc in next 2 sts, sc in next 3 sts] 5 times, 2 sc in next 2 sts, sc in next 2 sts, join to first sc made. End Color D. (22 sts)

ROUND 5: Join Color E, ch 1 and sc in same place, sc in next st, [2 sc in next 2 sts, sc in next 5 sts] 5 times, 2 sc in next 2 sts, sc in next 3 sts, join to first sc made. End Color E. (54 sts)

ROUND 6: Join Color F, ch 1 and sc in same place, sc in next 2 sts, [2 sc in next 2 sts, sc in next 7 sts] 5 times, 2 sc in next 2 sts, sc in next 4 sts, join to first sc made. End Color F. (66 sts)

ROUND 7: Join Color A, ch 3 (counts as 1 dc), dc in next 3 sts, [2 dc in next 2 sts, dc in next 9 sts] 5 times, 2 dc in next 2 sts, dc in next 5 sts, join to top of beginning ch. End Color A. (78 sts)

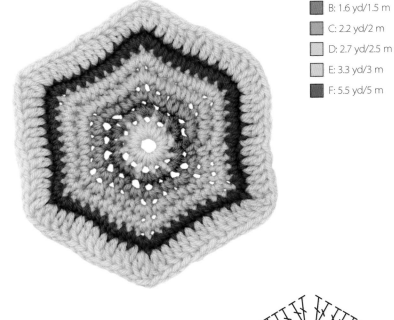

A: 10.4 yd/9.5 m
B: 1.6 yd/1.5 m
C: 2.2 yd/2 m
D: 2.7 yd/2.5 m
E: 3.3 yd/3 m
F: 5.5 yd/5 m

○   ch
•   sl st
+   sc
┬   dc
►   start of round

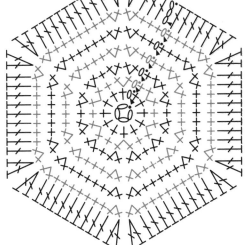

Windmill

• **SKILL LEVEL:** Beginner
• **SIZE OF HEXAGON:** 7 in. (18 cm)

Method

FOUNDATION RING: With Color A, ch 4 and join to form a ring.

ROUND 1: Ch 1, 12 sc into ring, join to top of first sc made. (12 sts)

ROUND 2: Ch 3 (counts as 1 dc), dc in same place, 2 dc in next 11 sts, join to top of beginning ch. End Color A. (24 sts)

ROUND 3: Join Color B, ch 6 (counts as 1 dc, ch 3), [skip 1 st, dc in next st, ch 3] 11 times, join to 3rd ch of beginning ch. (12 sts, 12 ch sp)

ROUND 4: Ch 6 (counts as 1 dc, ch 3), * dc in ch-3 sp, dc in next st, dc in next ch-3 sp, ch 3 **, dc in next st, ch 3; rep from * 4 more times, then from * to ** once, join to 3rd ch of beginning ch. End Color B. (24 sts, 12 ch sp)

ROUND 5: Join Color C, ch 6 (counts as 1 dc, ch 3), * dc in ch-3 sp, dc in next 3 sts, dc in next ch-3 sp, ch 3 **, dc in next st, ch 3; rep from * 4 more times, then from * to ** once, join to 3rd ch of beginning ch. (36 sts, 12 ch sp)

ROUND 6: Ch 6 (counts as 1 dc, ch 3), * dc in ch-3 sp, dc in next 5 sts, dc in next ch-3 sp, ch 3 **, dc in next st, ch 3; rep from * 4 more times, then from * to ** once, join to 3rd ch of beginning ch. End Color C. (48 sts, 12 ch sp)

A: 4.4 yd/4 m
B: 7.1 yd/6.5 m
C: 13.7 yd/12.5 m

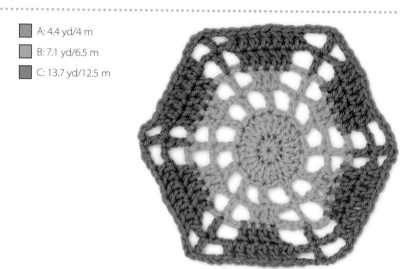

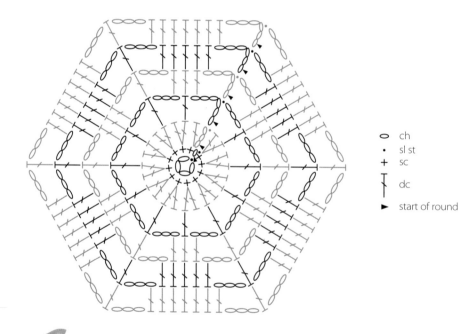

○ ch
• sl st
+ sc
| dc
► start of round

Wheel

- **SKILL LEVEL:** Beginner
- **SIZE OF HEXAGON:** 7 in. (18 cm)

o   ch
·   sl st
+   sc
╪   dc
►   start of round

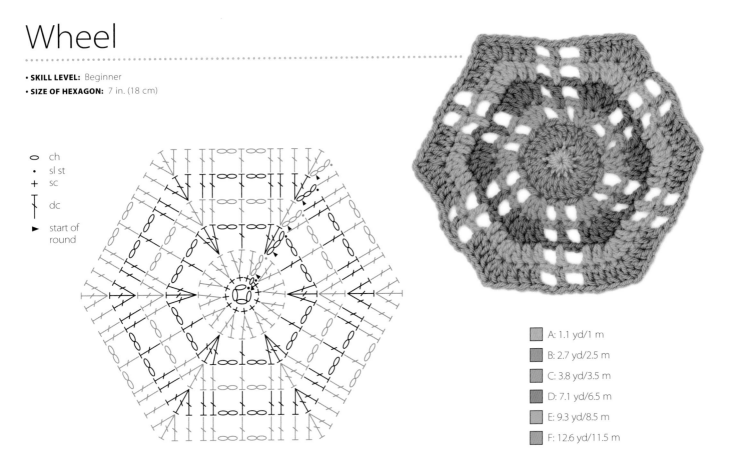

A: 1.1 yd/1 m
B: 2.7 yd/2.5 m
C: 3.8 yd/3.5 m
D: 7.1 yd/6.5 m
E: 9.3 yd/8.5 m
F: 12.6 yd/11.5 m

Method

FOUNDATION RING: With Color A, ch 4 and join to form a ring.

ROUND 1: Ch 1, 12 sc into ring, join to first sc made. End Color A. (12 sts)

ROUND 2: Join Color B, ch 3 (counts as 1 dc), dc in same place, 2 dc in next 11 sts, join to top of beginning ch. End Color B. (24 sts)

ROUND 3: Join Color C, ch 3 (counts as 1 dc), 2 dc in same place, * ch 2, skip 1 st, dc in next st, ch 2, skip 1 st **, 3 dc in next st; rep from * 4 more times, then from * to ** once, join to top of beginning ch. End Color C. (24 sts, 12 ch sp)

ROUND 4: Join Color D in next st, ch 3 (counts as 1 dc), 2 dc in same place, * [dc in next st, ch 2, skip ch sp] twice, dc in next st **, 3 dc in next st; rep from * 4 more times, then from * to ** once, join to top of beginning ch. End Color D. (36 sts, 12 ch sp)

ROUND 5: Join Color E in next st, ch 3 (counts as 1 dc), 2 dc in same place, * dc in next 2 sts, ch 2, skip ch sp, dc in next st, ch 2, skip ch sp, dc in next 2 sts **, 3 dc in next st; rep from * 4 more times, then from * to ** once, join to top of beginning ch. End Color E. (48 sts, 12 ch sp)

ROUND 6: Join Color F in next st, ch 3 (counts as 1 dc), 2 dc in same place, * dc in next 3 sts, ch 2, skip ch sp, dc in next st, ch 2, skip ch sp, dc in next 3 sts **, 3 dc in next st; rep from * 4 more times, then from * to ** once, join to top of beginning ch. End Color F. (60 sts, 12 ch sp)

Spectrum

- **SKILL LEVEL:** Beginner
- **SIZE OF HEXAGON:** 5 in. (13 cm)

Method

FOUNDATION RING: With Color A, make a magic ring.

ROUND 1: Ch 1, 6 sc into ring, join to first sc made. End Color A. (6 sts)

ROUND 2: Join Color B, ch 1, 2 sc in each st, join to first sc made. End Color B. (12 sts)

ROUND 3: Join Color C, ch 1, (sc, ch 1, sc) in same place, [sc in next st, (sc, ch 1, sc) in next st] 5 times, sc in next st, join to first sc made. End Color C. (18 sts, 6 ch sp)

ROUND 4: Join Color D in ch-1 sp, ch 1, [(sc, ch 1, sc) in ch-1 sp, ch 1, skip 1 st, sc in next st, ch 1, skip 1 st] 6 times, join to first sc made. End Color D. (18 sts, 18 ch sp)

ROUND 5: Join Color E in ch-1 sp, ch 1, [(sc, ch 1, sc) in ch-1 sp, (ch 1, skip 1 st, sc in ch-1 sp) twice, ch 1] 6 times, join to first sc made. End Color E. (24 sts, 24 ch sp)

ROUND 6: Join Color F in ch-1 sp, ch 1, [(sc, ch 1, sc) in ch-1 sp, (ch 1, skip 1 st, sc in ch-1 sp) 3 times, ch 1] 6 times, join to first sc made. End Color F. (30 sts, 30 ch sp)

ROUND 7: Join Color G in ch-1 sp, ch 1, [(sc, ch 1, sc) in ch-1 sp, (ch 1, skip 1 st, sc in ch-1 sp) 4 times, ch 1] 6 times, join to first sc made. End Color G. (36 sts, 36 ch sp)

ROUND 8: Join Color A in ch-1 sp, ch 1, [(sc, ch 1, sc) in ch-1 sp, (ch 1, skip 1 st, sc in ch-1 sp) 5 times, ch 1] 6 times, join to first sc made. End Color A. (42 sts, 42 ch sp)

ROUND 9: Join Color B in ch-1 sp, ch 1, [(sc, ch 1, sc) in ch-1 sp, (ch 1, skip 1 st, sc in ch-1 sp) 6 times, ch 1] 6 times, join to first sc made. End Color B. (48 sts, 48 ch sp)

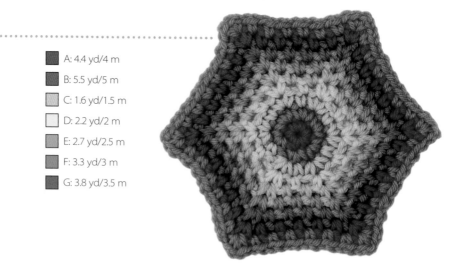

A: 4.4 yd/4 m
B: 5.5 yd/5 m
C: 1.6 yd/1.5 m
D: 2.2 yd/2 m
E: 2.7 yd/2.5 m
F: 3.3 yd/3 m
G: 3.8 yd/3.5 m

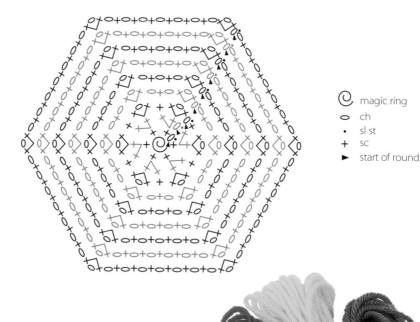

- ⊚ magic ring
- ○ ch
- • sl st
- + sc
- ► start of round

Pastel Bands

- **SKILL LEVEL:** Beginner
- **SIZE OF HEXAGON:** 7 in. (18 cm)

A: 7.1 yd/6.5 m
B: 13.7 yd/12.5 m
C: 7.1 yd/6.5 m
D: 5.5 yd/5 m

Method

FOUNDATION ROW: With Color A, ch 2.
ROW 1: 3 sc in 2nd ch from hook, turn. (3 sts)
ROW 2: Ch 1, 2 sc in first st, sc in next st, 2 sc in last st, turn. (5 sts)
ROW 3: Ch 1, 2 sc in first st, sc in each st to last, 2 sc in last st, turn. (7 sts)
ROWS 4–10: Repeat Row 3. (21 sts)
ROW 11: Ch 1, sc in each st to end, turn. End Color A. (21 sts)
ROW 12: Join Color B, ch 1, sc in each st to end, turn.
ROWS 13–21: Repeat Row 12. End Color B.
ROW 22: Join Color C, ch 1, sc in each st to end, turn.
ROW 23: Ch 1, sc2tog, sc in each st to last 2 sts, sc2tog, turn. (19 sts)
ROWS 24–31: Repeat Row 23. (3 sts)
ROW 32: Ch 1, sc3tog. End Color C. (1 st)

EDGING
Join Color D in same place and work (ch 1, sc, hdc, sc) in same place, [sc in 10 row edges, (sc, hdc, sc) in next row edge] 5 times, sc in 10 row edges, join to first sc made. End Color D. (78 sts)

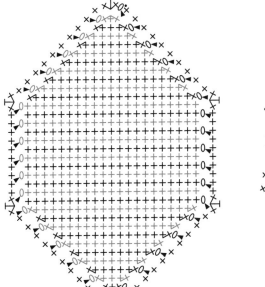

○   ch
•   sl st
+   sc
T   hdc
✕✕   sc2tog
✕⁺✕   sc3tog
▶   start of row or round

Europa

- **SKILL LEVEL:** Beginner
- **SIZE OF HEXAGON:** 7 in. (18 cm)

Method

FOUNDATION RING: With Color A, make a magic ring.

ROUND 1: Ch 1, 6 sc into ring, join to first sc made. End Color A. (6 sts)

ROUND 2: Join Color B, ch 1, 2 sc in each st, join to first sc made. End Color B. (12 sts)

ROUND 3: Join Color C, ch 2 (counts as 1 hdc), hdc in same place, [hdc in next st, 2 hdc in next st] 5 times, hdc in next st, join to top of beginning ch. End Color C. (18 sts)

ROUND 4: Join Color D, ch 3 (counts as 1 dc), [dc in next st, 2 dc in next st, dc in next st] 5 times, dc in next st, 2 dc in next st, join to top of beginning ch. End Color D. (24 sts)

ROUND 5: Join Color E, ch 3 (counts as 1 dc), [2 dc in next st, dc in next 3 sts] 5 times, 2 dc in next st, dc in next 2 sts, join to top of beginning ch. End Color E. (30 sts)

ROUND 6: Join Color F, ch 2 (counts as 1 hdc), * sc in next 2 sts, hdc in next st, 3 dc in next st ** , hdc in next st; rep from * 4 more times, then from * to ** once, join to top of beginning ch. End Color F. (42 sts)

ROUND 7: Join Color G, ch 3 (counts as 1 dc), dc in next 4 sts, [3 dc in next st, dc in next 6 sts] 5 times, 3 dc in next st, dc in next st, join to top of beginning ch. End Color G. (54 sts)

ROUND 8: Join Color C, ch 1 and sc in same place, sc in next 5 sts, [(sc, hdc, sc) in next st, sc in next 8 sts] 5 times, (sc, hdc, sc) in next st, sc in next 2 sts, join to first sc made. End Color C. (66 sts)

A: 1.1 yd/1 m
B: 1.1 yd/1 m
C: 2.2 yd/2 m
D: 2.2 yd/2 m
E: 11 yd/10 m
F: 9.8 yd/9 m
G: 15.3 yd/14 m

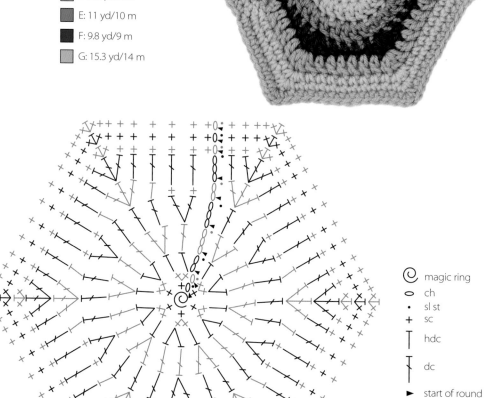

⟲ magic ring
○ ch
• sl st
+ sc
T hdc
T dc
► start of round

ROUND 9: Join Color D, ch 1 and sc in same place, sc in next 6 sts, [(sc, hdc, sc) in next st, sc in next 10 sts] 5 times, (sc, hdc, sc) in next st, sc in next 3 sts, join to first sc made. End Color D. (78 sts)

ROUND 10: Join Color G, ch 1 and sc in same place, sc in next 7 sts, [(sc, hdc, sc) in next st, sc in next 12 sts] 5 times, (sc, hdc, sc) in next st, sc in next 4 sts, join to first sc made. End Color G. (90 sts)

Redshift

- **SKILL LEVEL:** Beginner
- **SIZE OF HEXAGON:** 7 in. (18 cm)

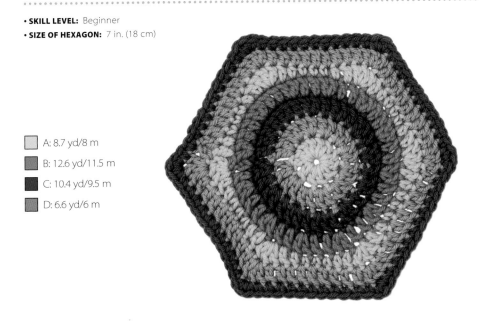

A: 8.7 yd/8 m

B: 12.6 yd/11.5 m

C: 10.4 yd/9.5 m

D: 6.6 yd/6 m

Method

FOUNDATION RING: With Color A, make a magic ring.

ROUND 1: Ch 3 (counts as 1 dc), 11 dc into ring, join to top of beginning ch. End Color A. (12 sts)

ROUND 2: Join Color B, ch 3 (counts as 1 dc), dc in same place, 2 dc in next 11 sts, join to top of beginning ch. End Color B. (24 sts)

ROUND 3: Join Color C, ch 3 (counts as 1 dc), dc in same place, [dc in next st, 2 dc in next st] 11 times, dc in next st, join to top of beginning ch. End Color C. (36 sts)

ROUND 4: Join Color D, ch 3 (counts as 1 dc), dc in next st, [2 dc in next st, dc in next 2 sts] 11 times, 2 dc in next st, join to top of beginning ch. End Color D. (48 sts)

ROUND 5: Join Color A, ch 3 (counts as 1 dc), 2 dc in same place, * dc in next st, hdc in next st, sc in next 3 sts, hdc in next st, dc in next st **, 3 dc in next st; rep from * 4 more times, then from * to ** once, join to top of beginning ch. End Color A. (60 sts)

ROUND 6: Join Color B, ch 3 (counts as 1 dc), [3 dc in next st, dc in next 9 sts] 5 times, 3 dc in next st, dc in next 8 sts, join to top of beginning ch. End Color B. (72 sts)

ROUND 7: Join Color C, ch 1 and sc in same place, sc in next st, [(sc, hdc, sc) in next st, sc in next 11 sts] 5 times, (sc, hdc, sc) in next st, sc in next 9 sts, join to first sc made. End Color A. (84 sts)

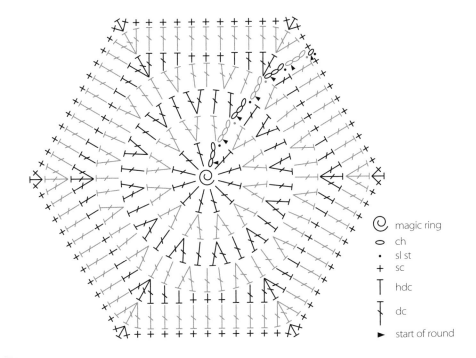

◉	magic ring
○	ch
•	sl st
+	sc
T	hdc
Ŧ	dc
►	start of round

Lace Flower

- **SKILL LEVEL:** Beginner
- **SIZE OF HEXAGON:** 7 in. (18 cm)

Method

FOUNDATION RING: With Color A, make a magic ring.

ROUND 1: Ch 1, [sc into ring, ch 3] 6 times, join to first sc made. End Color A. (6 sts, 6 ch sp)

ROUND 2: Join Color B in ch-3 sp, ch 4 (counts as 1 dc, ch 1), dc in same place, [ch 1, (dc, ch 1, dc) in next ch-3 sp] 5 times, ch 1, join to top of beginning ch. (12 sts, 12 ch sp)

ROUND 3: Sl st into ch-1 sp, ch 3 (counts as 1 dc), 2 dc in same place, [3 dc in next ch-1 sp] 11 times, join to top of beginning ch. End Color B. (36 sts)

ROUND 4: Join Color C, ch 3 (counts as 1 dc), dc in next 5 sts, [ch 2, dc in next 6 sts] 5 times, ch 2, join to top of beginning ch. (36 sts, 6 ch sp)

ROUND 5: Ch 2, dc in next st (decrease made), * dc in next 2 sts, dc2tog, ch 4, sc in ch-2 sp, ch 4 **, dc2tog; rep from * 4 more times, then from * to ** once, join to first decreased dc made. End Color C. (30 sts, 12 ch sp)

ROUND 6: Join Color D, ch 2, dc in next st (decrease made), * dc2tog, [ch 4, sc in ch-4 sp] twice, ch 4 **, dc2tog; rep from * 4 more times, then from * to ** once, join to first decreased dc made. End Color D. (24 sts, 18 ch sp)

ROUND 7: Join Color A, ch 1, [sc2tog, (ch 4, sc in next sc) twice, ch 4] 6 times, join to first decreased sc made. End Color A. (18 sts, 18 ch sp)

A: 6.6 yd/6 m

B: 6.6 yd/6 m

C: 10.4 yd/9.5 m

D: 6 yd/5.5 m

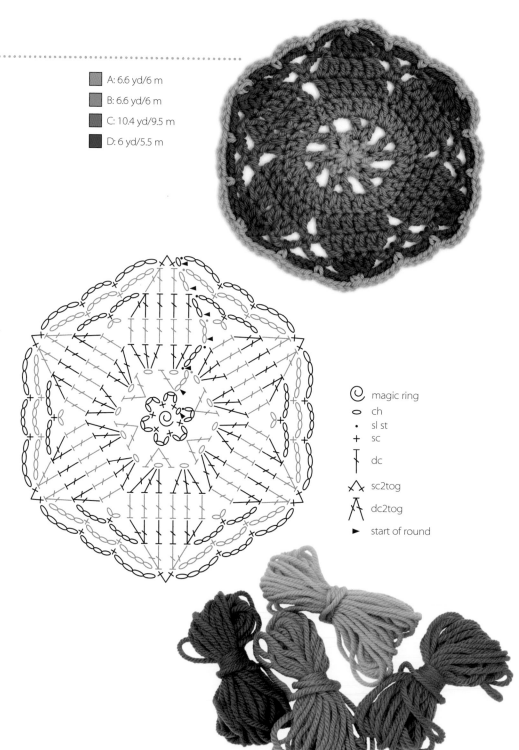

magic ring

ch

sl st

sc

dc

sc2tog

dc2tog

start of round

Radar

- **SKILL LEVEL:** Beginner
- **SIZE OF HEXAGON:** 7 in. (18 cm)

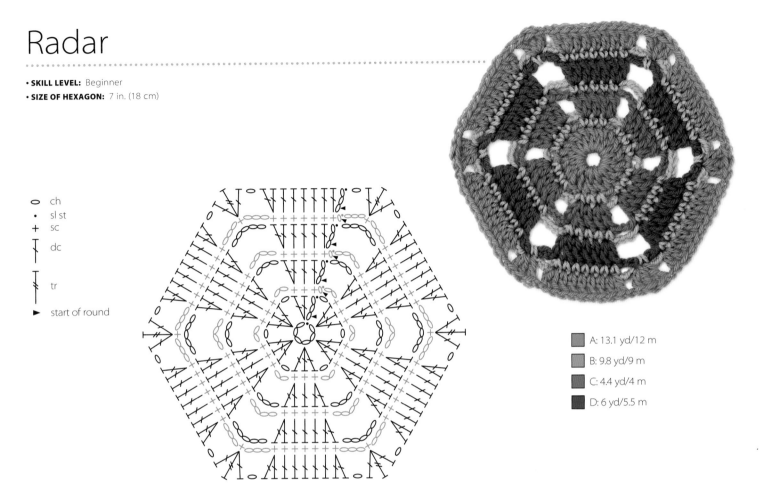

○ ch
• sl st
+ sc
† dc
‡ tr
► start of round

A: 13.1 yd/12 m
B: 9.8 yd/9 m
C: 4.4 yd/4 m
D: 6 yd/5.5 m

Method

FOUNDATION RING: With Color A, ch 6 and join to form a ring.

ROUND 1: Ch 3 (counts as 1 dc), 2 dc into ring, [ch 1, 3 dc into ring] 5 times, ch 1, join to top of beginning ch. End Color A. (18 sts, 6 ch sp)

ROUND 2: Join Color B, ch 1, [sc in next 3 sts, ch 2] 6 times, join to first sc made. End Color B. (18 sts, 6 ch sp)

ROUND 3: Join Color C, ch 3 (counts as 1 dc), dc in same place, * dc in next st, 2 dc in next st, ch 3, skip ch-2 sp **, 2 dc in next st; rep from * 4 more times, then from * to ** once, join to top of beginning ch. End Color C. (30 sts, 6 ch sp)

ROUND 4: Join Color B, ch 1, [sc in next 5 sts, ch 4] 6 times, join to first sc made. End Color B. (30 sts, 6 ch sp)

ROUND 5: Join Color D, ch 3 (counts as 1 dc), dc in same place, * dc in next 3 sts, 2 dc in next st, ch 5, skip ch-3 sp **, 2 dc in next st; rep from * 4 more times, then from * to ** once, join to top of beginning ch. End Color D. (42 sts, 6 ch sp)

ROUND 6: Join Color B, ch 1, [sc in next 7 sts, ch 3, sc in ch-5 sp, ch 3] 6 times, join to first sc made. End Color B. (48 sts, 12 ch sp)

ROUND 7: Join Color A, ch 3 (counts as 1 dc), dc in same place, * dc in next 5 sts, 2 dc in next st, ch 1, (dc, tr, dc) in next sc, ch 1 **, 2 dc in next st; rep from * 4 more times, then from * to ** once, join to top of beginning ch. End Color A. (72 sts, 12 ch sp)

PROJECT
Baby Blanket

- **SKILL LEVEL:** Beginner
- **SIZE OF HEXAGON:** 5 in. (13 cm)
- **FINISHED SIZE:** 44 in. (112 cm) at widest point
- **HOOK SIZE:** H (5 mm)
- **YARN WEIGHT:** DK/light worsted

A: 221.5 yd/202.5 m
B: 289 yd/264 m
C: 239.5 yd/219 m
D: 131.5 yd/120 m

E: 131.5 yd/120 m
F: 157.5 yd/144 m
G: 131.5 yd/120 m

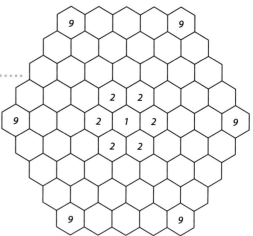

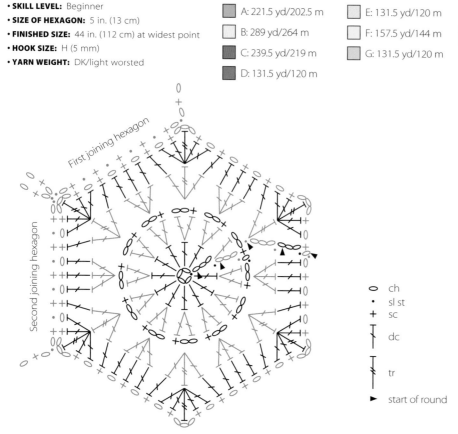

First joining hexagon

Second joining hexagon

○ ch
• sl st
+ sc
┬ dc
╫ tr
► start of round

HEXAGON COLORWAYS
Make the foundation ring using the same color as Round 1 and change colors on each round as follows:
HEXAGON 1 (MAKE 1): 1–5A, 6B.
HEXAGON 2 (MAKE 6): 1–5C, 6B.
HEXAGON 3 (MAKE 8): 1–2C, 3B, 4–5D, 6B.
HEXAGON 4 (MAKE 8): 1–2D, 3B, 4–5C, 6B.
HEXAGON 5 (MAKE 8): 1–2E, 3B, 4–5F, 6B.
HEXAGON 6 (MAKE 8): 1–2F, 3B, 4–5E, 6B.
HEXAGON 7 (MAKE 8): 1–2G, 3B, 4–5A, 6B.
HEXAGON 8 (MAKE 8): 1–2A, 3B, 4–5G, 6B.
HEXAGON 9 (MAKE 6): 1–2F, 3B, 4–5A, 6B.

Method

Make 61 hexagons in the specified colorways as follows:
FOUNDATION RING: Ch 4 and join to form a ring.
ROUND 1: Ch 3 (counts as 1 dc), 11 dc into ring, join to top of beginning ch. (12 sts)
ROUND 2: Ch 3 (counts as 1 dc), dc in same place, [2 dc in next st] 11 times, join to top of beginning ch. (24 sts)
ROUND 3: Ch 1 and sc in same place, [ch 2, skip 1 st, sc in next st] 11 times, ch 2, join to first sc made. (12 sts, 12 ch sp)
ROUND 4: Sl st into ch-2 sp, ch 3 (counts as 1 dc), (tr, dc) in same place, [3 dc in next ch-2 sp, (dc, tr, dc) in next ch-2 sp] 5 times, 3 dc in next ch-2 sp, join to top of beginning ch. (36 sts)

ROUND 5: Ch 3 (counts as 1 dc), * (2 dc, tr, 2 dc) in next st **, dc in next 5 sts; rep from * 4 more times, then from * to ** once, dc in next 4 sts, join to top of beginning ch. (60 sts)

FIRST HEXAGON ONLY
ROUND 6: Ch 1 and sc in same place, ch 1, skip 1 st, * sc in next st, ch 3, skip 1 st **, [sc in next st, ch 1, skip 1 st] 4 times; rep from * 4 more times, then from * to ** once, [sc in next st, ch 1, skip 1 st] 3 times, join to first sc made. (30 sts, 30 ch sp)

ALL REMAINING HEXAGONS
Work Rounds 1–5 as for first hexagon, then join together on Round 6 using the join-as-you-go technique (see page 137). Follow the layout diagram for hexagons 1, 2, and 9, and randomly place hexagons 3–8. Where two hexagons join along a side edge, work a sl st into the corresponding ch sp on the adjoining hexagon instead of working a ch. At each corner, work (ch 1, sl st into ch sp on adjoining hexagon(s), ch 1).

Shawl

. . . .

- **SKILL LEVEL:** Beginner
- **SIZE OF HEXAGON:** 6 in. (15 cm)
- **FINISHED SIZE:** 69 x 23 in. (176 x 58 cm)
- **HOOK SIZE:** G (4 mm)
- **YARN WEIGHT:** Fingering

▪	A: 64.5 yd/59 m	▪	E: 49.5 yd/45 m
▪	B: 265.5 yd/242.5 m	▪	F: 46.5 yd/42.5 m
▪	C: 92 yd/84 m	▪	G: 49.5 yd/45 m
▪	D: 163.5 yd/149.5 m	▪	H: 46.5 yd/42.5 m

HEXAGON COLORWAYS

Make the foundation ring using the same color as Round 1 and change colors on each round as follows:

HEXAGON 1 (MAKE 5): 1A, 2A, 3B, 4C, 5D, 6A, 7B.
HEXAGON 2 (MAKE 6): 1G, 2G, 3B, 4C, 5D, 6E, 7B.
HEXAGON 3 (MAKE 3): 1H, 2H, 3B, 4C, 5D, 6F, 7B.
HEXAGON 4 (MAKE 4): 1E, 2E, 3B, 4C, 5D, 6G, 7B.
HEXAGON 5 (MAKE 4): 1F, 2F, 3B, 4C, 5D, 6H, 7B.

Make the following hexagons as above but use Color D instead of B on Round 7.

HEXAGON 1 (MAKE 2)
HEXAGON 3 (MAKE 2)
HEXAGON 4 (MAKE 1)
HEXAGON 5 (MAKE 1)

Method

Make 28 hexagons in the specified colorways as follows:

FOUNDATION RING: Ch 4 and join to form a ring.
ROUND 1: Ch 1, 9 sc into ring, join to first sc made. (9 sts)
ROUND 2: Ch 3 (counts as 1 dc), dc in same place, [2 dc in next st] 8 times, join to top of beginning ch. (18 sts)
ROUND 3: Ch 3 (counts as 1 dc), dc in next 2 sts, [ch 3, dc in next 3 sts] 5 times, ch 3, join to top of beginning ch. (18 sts, 6 ch sp)

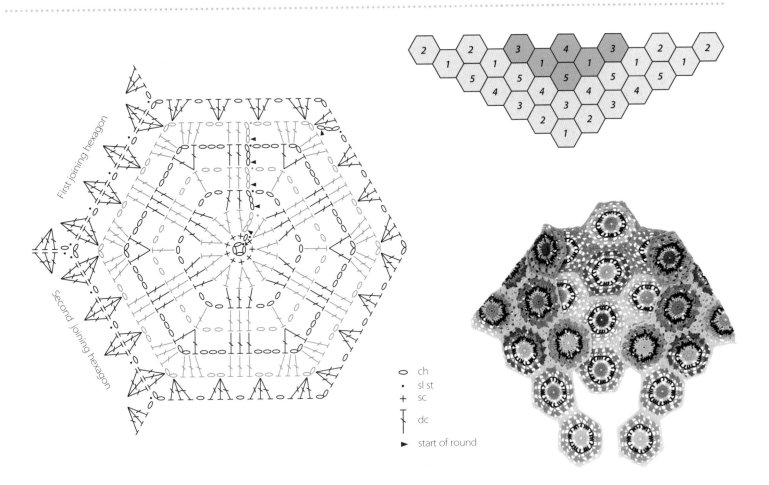

First joining hexagon

Second joining hexagon

○	ch
•	sl st
+	sc
⊺	dc
►	start of round

ROUND 4: Ch 3 (counts as 1 dc), dc in next 2 sts, [ch 2, dc in ch-3 sp, ch 2, dc in next 3 sts] 5 times, ch 2, dc in ch-3 sp, ch 2, join to top of beginning ch. (24 sts, 12 ch sp)

ROUND 5: Ch 3 (counts as 1 dc), dc in next 2 sts, [ch 3, (dc, ch 2, dc) in next st, ch 3, dc in next 3 sts] 5 times, ch 3, (dc, ch 2, dc) in next st, ch 3, join to top of beginning ch. (30 sts, 18 ch sp)

ROUND 6: Ch 3 (counts as 1 dc), dc in next 2 sts, [ch 2, dc in next st, (2 dc, ch 2, 2 dc) in ch-2 sp, dc in next st, ch 2, dc in next 3 sts] 5 times, ch 2, dc in next st, (2 dc, ch 2, 2 dc) in ch-2 sp, dc in

next st, ch 2, join to top of beginning ch. (54 sts, 18 ch sp)

FIRST HEXAGON ONLY

ROUND 7: Join new color in corner ch-2 sp, ch 3 (counts as 1 dc), (2 dc, ch 2, 3 dc) in same place, [ch 1, (3 dc in next ch-2 sp, ch 1) twice, (3 dc, ch 2, 3 dc) in corner ch-2 sp] 5 times, [ch 1, 3 dc in next ch-2 sp] twice, ch 1, join to top of beginning ch. (72 sts, 24 ch sp)

ALL REMAINING HEXAGONS

Work Rounds 1–6 as for first hexagon, then join together on Round 7 using the join-as-you-go method (see page 137). Follow the layout diagram, positioning the hexagons edged in Color D at the center top as indicated. Where two hexagons join along a side edge, work a sl st into the corresponding ch sp of the adjoining hexagon instead of working a ch. At each corner, work a sl st into the corner ch sp of the adjoining hexagon(s) in place of one ch.

Sunshine

- **SKILL LEVEL:** Intermediate
- **SIZE OF HEXAGON:** 7 in. (18 cm)

SPECIAL STITCHES:
Beg CL: Beginning cluster made of ch 3, 3 dc.
CL: Cluster made of 4 dc.

Method

FOUNDATION RING: With Color A, ch 4 and join to form a ring.

ROUND 1: Ch 3 (counts as 1 dc), 11 dc into ring, join to top of beginning ch. End Color A. (12 sts)

ROUND 2: Join Color B, ch 5 (counts as 1 tr, ch 1), tr in same place, (tr, ch 1, tr) in next 11 sts, join to 4th ch of beginning ch. End Color B. (24 sts, 12 ch sp)

ROUND 3: Join Color C in ch-1 sp, beg CL, [ch 4, skip 2 sts, CL in next ch-1 sp] 11 times, ch 4, join to top of beg CL. End Color C. (12 CL, 12 ch sp)

ROUND 4: Join Color D in top of beg CL, ch 1 and sc in same place, * 2 dc in space between skipped sts of Round 2, sc in next CL, (dc in space between skipped sts of Round 2, ch 3, dc in same place) **, sc in next CL; rep from * 4 more times, then from * to ** once, join to first sc made. (36 sts, 6 ch sp)

ROUND 5: Ch 3 (counts as 1 dc), [dc in each st to corner ch-3 sp, (3 dc, ch 3, 3 dc) in corner ch-3 sp] 6 times, dc in next st, join to top of beginning ch. End Color D. (54 sts, 6 ch sp)

ROUND 6: Join Color E, ch 1 and sc in same place, [sc in each st to corner ch-3 sp, (sc, hdc, sc) in corner ch-3 sp] 6 times, sc in next 4 sts, join to first sc made. End Color E. (90 sts)

ROUND 7: Join Color F, ch 1 and sc in same place, [sc in each st to corner hdc, (sc, hdc, sc) in corner hdc] 6 times, sc in next 5 sts, join to first sc made. End Color F. (102 sts)

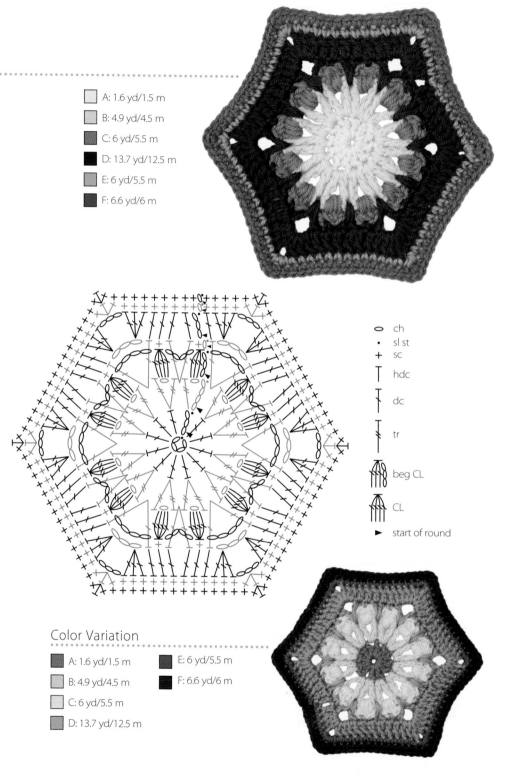

A:	1.6 yd/1.5 m
B:	4.9 yd/4.5 m
C:	6 yd/5.5 m
D:	13.7 yd/12.5 m
E:	6 yd/5.5 m
F:	6.6 yd/6 m

⬭	ch
•	sl st
+	sc
T	hdc
⊤	dc
⧗	tr
	beg CL
	CL
►	start of round

Color Variation

A: 1.6 yd/1.5 m		E: 6 yd/5.5 m	
B: 4.9 yd/4.5 m		F: 6.6 yd/6 m	
C: 6 yd/5.5 m			
D: 13.7 yd/12.5 m			

Victorian Paper Flower

- **SKILL LEVEL:** Intermediate
- **SIZE OF HEXAGON:** 7 in. (18 cm)

- A: 3.8 yd/3.5 m
- B: 7.1 yd/6.5 m
- C: 10.4 yd/9.5 m
- D: 16.4 yd/15 m
- E: 6 yd/5.5 m

Method

FOUNDATION RING: With Color A, ch 4 and join to form a ring.

ROUND 1: Ch 3 (counts as 1 dc), 11 dc into ring, join to top of beginning ch. (12 sts)

ROUND 2: Ch 1, [sc tfl, ch 3] 12 times, join to first sc made. End Color A. (12 sts, 12 ch sp)

ROUND 3: Join Color B tbl, ch 3 (counts as 1 dc), dc tbl in same place, 2 dc tbl in each st around, join to top of beginning ch. (24 sts)

ROUND 4: Ch 1, [sc tfl, ch 3] 24 times, join to first sc made. End Color B. (24 sts, 24 ch sp)

ROUND 5: Join Color C tbl, ch 3 (counts as 1 dc), dc tbl in same place, [dc tbl in next st, 2 dc tbl in next st] 11 times, dc tbl in next st, join to top of beginning ch. (36 sts)

ROUND 6: Ch 1, [sc tfl, ch 3] 36 times, join to first sc made. End Color C. (36 sts, 36 ch sp)

ROUND 7: Join Color D tbl, ch 3 (counts as 1 dc), * (2 tr tbl, ch 2, 2 tr tbl) in next st, dc tbl in next st, hdc tbl in next st, sc tbl in next st, hdc tbl in next st **, dc tbl in next st; rep from * 4 more times, then from * to ** once, join to top of beginning ch. (54 sts, 6 ch sp)

ROUND 8: Ch 3, [dc in each st to corner ch-2 sp, (dc, ch 1, dc) in ch-2 sp] 6 times, dc in next 6 sts, join to top of beginning ch. End Color D. (66 sts, 6 ch sp)

ROUND 9: Join Color E, ch 1 and sc in same place, [sc in each st to corner ch-1 sp, (sc, hdc, sc) in ch-1 sp] 6 times, sc in next 7 sts, join to first sc made. End Color E. (84 sts)

- O ch
- • sl st
- + sc
- ⊤ hdc
- ⊤ dc
- ⚓ sc tfl
- ⊼ sc tbl
- ⊤ hdc tbl
- ⊻ dc tbl
- ⊤ tr tbl
- ► start of round

Color Variation

- A: 3.8 yd/3.5 m
- B: 7.1 yd/6.5 m
- C: 10.4 yd/9.5 m
- D: 16.4 yd/15 m
- E: 6 yd/5.5 m

Frosty Candy

- **SKILL LEVEL:** Intermediate
- **SIZE OF HEXAGON:** 5 in. (13 cm)

☐	A: 2.2 yd/2 m
☐	B: 8.2 yd/7.5 m
☐	C: 4.4 yd/4 m
☐	D: 6 yd/5.5 m

SPECIAL STITCHES:

Beg PC: Beginning popcorn made of ch 3, 4 dc.

PC: Popcorn made of 5 dc.

Method

FOUNDATION RING: With Color A, ch 4 and join to form a ring.

ROUND 1: Ch 3 (counts as 1 dc), 11 dc into ring, join to top of beginning ch. End Color A. (12 sts)

ROUND 2: Join Color B, beg PC in same place, [ch 2, PC in next st] 11 times, ch 2, join to top of beg PC. End Color B. (12 PC, 12 ch sp)

ROUND 3: Join Color C in next ch-2 sp, ch 3 (counts as 1 dc), 2 dc in same place, [ch 1, 3 dc in next ch-2 sp] 11 times, ch 1, join to top of beginning ch. End Color C. (36 sts, 12 ch sp)

ROUND 4: Join Color D tbl, ch 3 (counts as 1 dc), * (dc tbl, ch 2, dc tbl) in next st, dc tbl in next st, dc tbl in next ch, dc tbl in next 3 sts, dc tbl in next ch **, dc tbl in next st; rep from * 4 more times, then from * to ** once, join to top of beginning ch. End Color D. (54 sts, 6 ch sp)

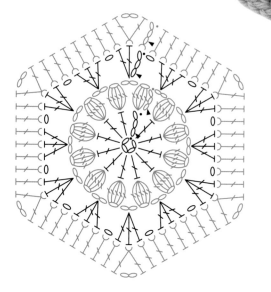

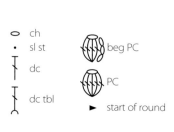

⬭	ch
•	sl st
╎	dc
╪	dc tbl
🮲	beg PC
🮲	PC
►	start of round

Color Variation 1

☐	A: 2.2 yd/2 m
☐	B: 8.2 yd/7.5 m
■	C: 4.4 yd/4 m
☐	D: 6 yd/5.5 m

Color Variation 2

☐	A: 2.2 yd/2 m
☐	B: 8.2 yd/7.5 m
☐	C: 4.4 yd/4 m
☐	D: 6 yd/5.5 m

Additional Variations

Alternate Colors A and C.

Dansk

- **SKILL LEVEL:** Intermediate
- **SIZE OF HEXAGON:** 7 in. (18 cm)

Method

FOUNDATION RING: With Color A, ch 4 and join to form a ring.

ROUND 1: Ch 1, 12 sc into ring, join to first sc made. End Color A. (12 sts)

ROUND 2: Join Color B, ch 1, 2 sc in each st around, join to first sc made. End Color B. (24 sts)

ROUND 3: Join Color C, ch 1, sc in same place, [ch 7, skip 3 sts, sc in next st] 5 times, ch 7, join to first sc made. (6 sts, 6 ch sp)

ROUND 4: Ch 1 and sc in same place, [7 sc in ch-7 sp, sc in next st] 5 times, 7 sc in ch-7 sp, join to first sc made. End Color C. (48 sts)

ROUND 5: Join Color A, ch 1 and sc in same place, sc in next 3 sts, * (sc, ch 1, sc) in next st **, sc in next 7 sts; rep from * 4 more times, then from * to ** once, sc in next 3 sts, join to first sc made. End Color A. (54 sts, 6 ch sp)

ROUND 6: Join Color D, ch 1 and sc in same place, sc in next 4 sts, * (sc, ch 1, sc) in ch-1 sp **, sc in next 9 sts; rep from * 4 more times, then from * to ** once, sc in next 4 sts, join to first sc made. End Color D. (66 sts, 6 ch sp)

ROUND 7: Join Color E in ch-1 sp, ch 5 (counts as 1 dc, ch 2), dc in same place, * [ch 1, skip 1 st, dc in next st] 5 times, ch 1, skip 1 st **, (dc , ch 2, dc) in ch-1 sp; rep from * 4 more times, then from * to ** once, join to 3rd ch of beginning ch. End Color E. (42 sts, 42 ch sp)

ROUND 8: Join Color B in ch-2 sp, ch 1, [(sc, ch 1, sc) in ch-2 sp, sc in each ch sp and st to next corner ch-2 sp] 6 times, join to first sc made. End Color B. (90 sts, 6 ch sp)

ROUND 9: Join Color C in ch-1 sp, ch 3 (counts as 1 dc), 2 dc in same place, dc in each st to corner ch-1 sp, 3 dc in corner sp] 5 times, dc in each st to start of round, join to top of beginning ch. End Color C. (108 sts)

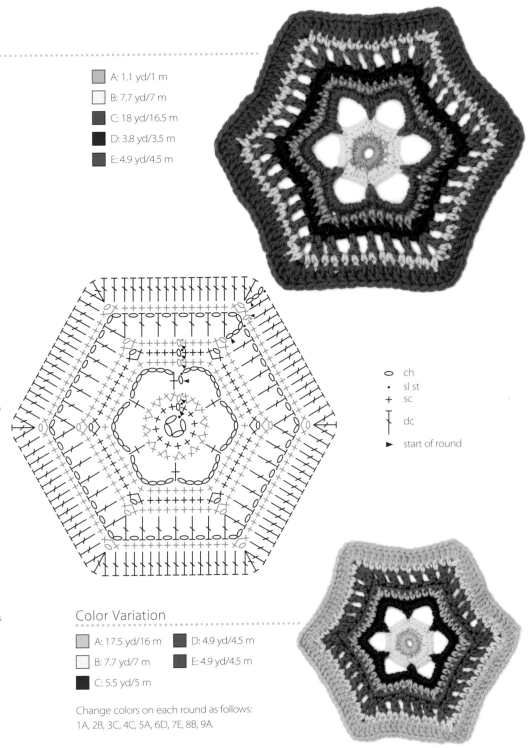

	A: 1.1 yd/1 m
	B: 7.7 yd/7 m
	C: 18 yd/16.5 m
	D: 3.8 yd/3.5 m
	E: 4.9 yd/4.5 m

o	ch
•	sl st
+	sc
†	dc
►	start of round

Color Variation

A: 17.5 yd/16 m	D: 4.9 yd/4.5 m
B: 7.7 yd/7 m	E: 4.9 yd/4.5 m
C: 5.5 yd/5 m	

Change colors on each round as follows:
1A, 2B, 3C, 4C, 5A, 6D, 7E, 8B, 9A.

Arabesque

- **SKILL LEVEL:** Intermediate
- **SIZE OF HEXAGON:** 7 in. (18 cm)

SPECIAL STITCHES:
Beg CL: Beginning cluster made of ch 3, 2 dc.
CL: Cluster made of 3 dc.

A: 1.6 yd/1.5 m
B: 4.9 yd/4.5 m
C: 16.4 yd/15 m
D: 8.2 yd/7.5 m
E: 9.8 yd/9 m

Method

FOUNDATION RING: With Color A, ch 4 and join to form a ring.

ROUND 1: Ch 3 (counts as 1 dc), 11 dc into ring, join to top of beginning ch. End Color A. (12 sts)

ROUND 2: Join Color B, beg CL in same place, [ch 3, CL in next st] 11 times, ch 3, join to top of beg CL. End Color B. (12 CL, 12 ch sp)

ROUND 3: Join Color C in next ch-3 sp, ch 1, [sc in ch-3 sp, ch 3] 12 times, join to first sc made. (12 sts, 12 ch sp)

ROUND 4: Sl st into next ch-3 sp, ch 1, [sc in ch-3 sp, ch 1, (2 dc, ch 2, 2 dc) in next ch-3 sp, ch 1] 6 times, join to first sc made. End Color C. (30 sts, 18 ch sp)

ROUND 5: Join Color D in previous ch-2 sp, ch 5 (counts as 1 dc, ch 2), dc in same place, * dc in next 2 sts, ch 2, sc in ch-1 sp, ch 3, sc in next ch-1 sp, ch 2, dc in next 2 sts **, (dc, ch 2, dc) in next ch-2 sp; rep from * 4 more times, then from * to ** once, join to 3rd ch of beginning ch. End Color D. (48 sts, 24 ch sp)

ROUND 6: Join Color E in next ch-2 sp, ch 5 (counts as 1 dc, ch 2), dc in same place, * dc in next 3 sts, ch 3, sc in next ch-3 sp, ch 3, dc in next 3 sts **, (dc, ch 2, dc) in next ch-2 sp; rep from * 4 more times, then from * to ** once, join to 3rd ch of beginning ch. End Color E. (54 sts, 18 ch sp)

ROUND 7: Join Color C in next ch-2 sp, ch 2 (counts as 1 hdc), (1 hdc, 1 dc, 2 hdc) in same place, * hdc in next 4 sts, ch 3, sc in next st, ch 3, hdc in next 4 sts **, (2 hdc, 1 dc, 2 hdc) in corner ch-2 sp; rep from * 4 more times, then from * to ** once, join to top of beginning ch. End Color C. (84 sts, 12 ch sp)

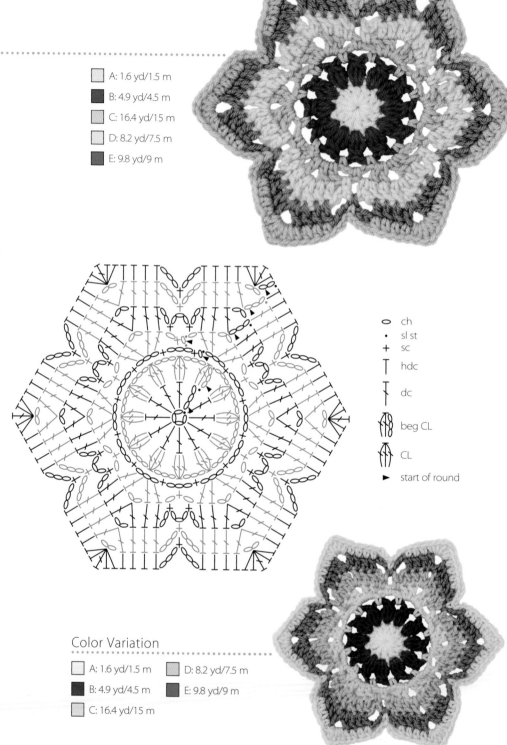

○ ch
• sl st
+ sc
T hdc
╪ dc
beg CL
CL
► start of round

Color Variation

A: 1.6 yd/1.5 m
B: 4.9 yd/4.5 m
C: 16.4 yd/15 m
D: 8.2 yd/7.5 m
E: 9.8 yd/9 m

Puff Flower

- **SKILL LEVEL:** Intermediate
- **SIZE OF HEXAGON:** 5 in. (13 cm)

SPECIAL STITCH:
PS: Puff stitch made of 5 hdc.

Method

FOUNDATION RING: With Color A, ch 4 and join to form a ring.
ROUND 1: Ch 1, 12 sc into ring, join to first sc made. End Color A. (12 sts)
ROUND 2: Join Color B, ch 3 (counts as 1 dc), dc in same place, 2 dc in next 11 sts, join to top of beginning ch. End Color B. (24 sts)
ROUND 3: Join Color C, ch 2, PS in same place, [ch 3, skip 1st st, PS in next st] 11 times, ch 3, join to top of first PS made. End Color C. (12 PS, 12 ch sp)
ROUND 4: Join Color D in previous ch-3 sp, ch 3 (counts as 1 dc), (2 dc, ch 2, 3 dc) in same place, [3 dc in next ch-3 sp, (3 dc, ch 2, 3 dc) in next ch-3 sp] 5 times, 3 dc in next ch-3 sp, join to top of beginning ch. End Color D. (54 sts, 6 ch sp)
ROUND 5: Join Color A in ch-2 sp, [3 sc in ch-2 sp, sc in next 9 sts] 6 times, join to first sc made. End Color A. (72 sts)

A: 6.6 yd/6 m
B: 2.7 yd/2.5 m
C: 6 yd/5.5 m
D: 7.1 yd/6.5 m

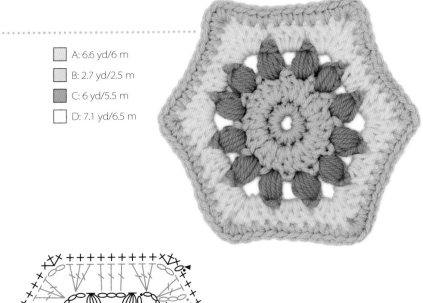
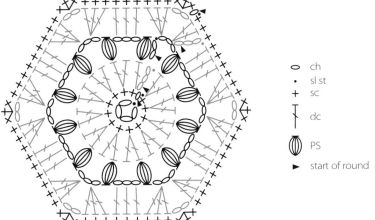

- ◯ ch
- • sl st
- + sc
- ⊤ dc
- ⬮ PS
- ► start of round

Color Variation 1

A: 6.6 yd/6 m
B: 2.7 yd/2.5 m
C: 6 yd/5.5 m
D: 7.1 yd/6.5 m

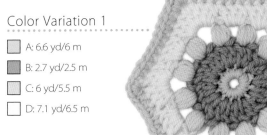
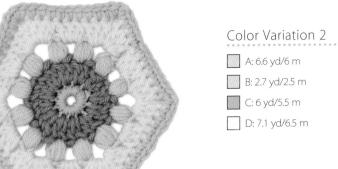

Color Variation 2

A: 6.6 yd/6 m
B: 2.7 yd/2.5 m
C: 6 yd/5.5 m
D: 7.1 yd/6.5 m

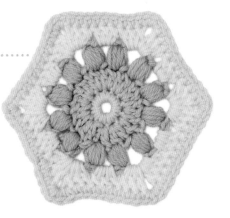

Folk Flower

- **SKILL LEVEL:** Intermediate
- **SIZE OF HEXAGON:** 7 in. (18 cm)

Method

FOUNDATION RING: With Color A, make a magic ring.

ROUND 1: Ch 1, 6 sc into ring, join to first sc made. End Color A. (6 sts)

ROUND 2: Join Color B, ch 1, 2 sc in each st, join to first sc made. End Color B. (12 sts)

ROUND 3: Join Color C, ch 1 and 2 sc in same place, 2 sc in each st around, join to first sc made. End Color C. (24 sts)

ROUND 4: Join Color D, [ch 2, (2 dc in next st) twice, ch 2, (sl st in next st) twice] 6 times. End Color D. (6 petals)

ROUND 5: Join Color E in sl st between two petals, ch 5 (counts as 1 dc, ch 2), dc in same place, [BPsc in next 4 sts, (dc, ch 2, dc) in next sl st between petals] 5 times, BPsc in next 4 sts, join to 3rd ch of beginning ch. (36 sts, 6 ch sp)

ROUND 6: Ch 3 (counts as 1 dc), [(2 dc, 1 tr, 2 dc) in ch-2 sp, dc in next 6 sts] 5 times, (2 dc, 1 tr, 2 dc) in next ch-2 sp, dc in next 5 sts, join to top of beginning ch. End Color E. (66 sts)

ROUND 7: With Color C, work standing BPsc in last st of Round 6, BPsc in next 2 sts, ch 2, skip 1 tr, [BPsc in next 10 sts, ch 2, skip 1 tr] 5 times, BPsc in next 7 sts, join to top of standing BPsc. End Color C. (60 sts, 6 ch sp)

ROUND 8: Join Color B in ch-2 sp, ch 1, [(sc, ch 2, sc) in ch-2 sp, BPsc in next 10 sts] 6 times, join to first sc made. End Color B. (72 sts, 6 ch sp)

ROUND 9: Join Color A in ch-2 sp, ch 3 (counts as 1 dc), 2 dc in same place, [BPdc in next 12 sts, 3 dc in ch-2 sp] 5 times, BPdc in next 12 sts, join to top of beginning ch. (90 sts, 6 ch sp)

ROUND 10: Ch 1 and sc in same place, [(sc, hdc, sc) in next st, sc in next 14 sts] 5 times, (sc, hdc, sc) in next st, sc in next 13 sts, join to first sc made. End Color A. (102 sts)

■	A: 19.7 yd/18 m
□	B: 6.6 yd/6 m
▨	C: 7.7 yd/7 m
□	D: 4.4 yd/4 m
▨	E: 12 yd/11 m

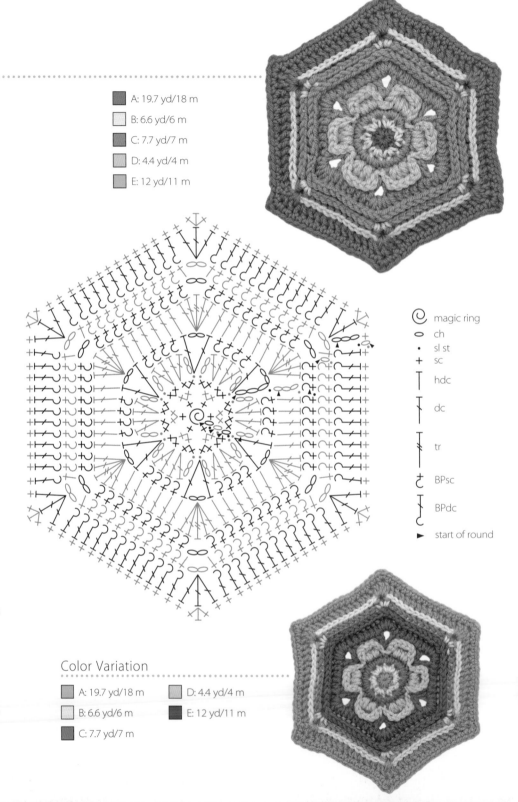

◉	magic ring
○	ch
•	sl st
+	sc
⊤	hdc
╫	dc
⟊	tr
⌇	BPsc
⌇	BPdc
▶	start of round

Color Variation

■ A: 19.7 yd/18 m		■ D: 4.4 yd/4 m	
□ B: 6.6 yd/6 m		■ E: 12 yd/11 m	
■ C: 7.7 yd/7 m			

Pop Flower

- **SKILL LEVEL:** Intermediate
- **SIZE OF HEXAGON:** 5 in. (13 cm)

SPECIAL STITCH:
CL: Cluster made of 5 tr.

A: 3.3 yd/3 m
B: 8.7 yd/8 m
C: 12 yd/11 m

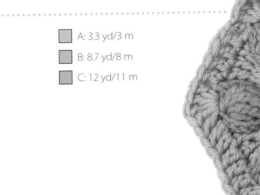

Method

FOUNDATION RING: With Color A, make a magic ring.

ROUND 1: Ch 1, 6 sc into ring, join to first sc made. (6 sts)

ROUND 2: Ch 1, 2 sc in next 6 sts, join to first sc made. (12 sts)

ROUND 3: Ch 1, [2 sc in next st, 1 sc in next st] 6 times, join to first sc made. End Color A. (18 sts)

ROUND 4: Join Color B, [(ch 6, CL, ch 6, sl st) in same place, ch 2, skip 1 st, sl st in next st] 6 times. End Color B. (6 petals, 6 ch sp)

ROUND 5: Join Color C in next ch-2 sp, ch 4 (counts as 1 tr), 4 tr in same place, [ch 2, skip CL, 5 tr in next ch-2 sp] 5 times, ch 2, join to top of beginning ch. (30 sts, 6 ch sp)

ROUND 6: Ch 3 (counts as 1 dc), [dc in each st to ch-2 sp, (2 dc, tr, 2 dc) in ch-2 sp] 6 times, join to top of beginning ch. End Color C. (60 sts)

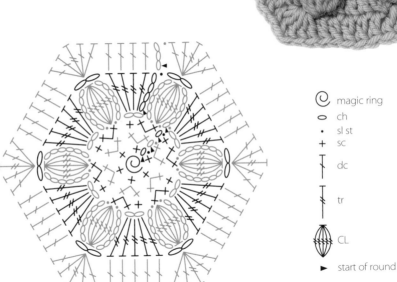

magic ring
ch
sl st
sc
dc
tr
CL
start of round

Color Variation 1

A: 3.3 yd/3 m
B: 8.7 yd/8 m
C: 12 yd/11 m

Color Variation 2

A: 3.3 yd/3 m
B: 8.7 yd/8 m
C: 12 yd/11 m

Cherry Blossom

- **SKILL LEVEL:** Intermediate
- **SIZE OF HEXAGON:** 7 in. (18 cm)

SPECIAL STITCHES:
Beg CL: Beginning cluster made of ch 2, 2 dc.
CL: Cluster made of 3 dc.

Method

FOUNDATION RING: With Color A, ch 5 and join to form a ring.

ROUND 1: Beg CL into ring, [ch 3, CL into ring] 5 times, ch 3, join to top of beg CL. End Color A. (6 CL, 6 ch sp)

ROUND 2: Join Color B in next ch-3 sp, ch 3 (counts as 1 dc), 4 dc in same place, [5 dc in next ch-3 sp] 5 times, join to top of beginning ch. End Color B. (30 sts)

ROUND 3: Join Color C, ch 3 (counts as 1 dc), dc in next st, * 2 dc in next st, dc in next 2 sts, dc into CL of Round 1 **, dc in next 2 sts; rep from * 4 more times, then from * to ** once, join to top of beginning ch. (42 sts)

ROUND 4: Ch 1 and sc in same place, * skip 2 sts, 7 dc in gap between 2 dc group, skip 2 sts **, sc in next 3 sts; rep from * 4 more times, then from * to ** once, sc in next 2 sts, join to first sc made. End Color C. (60 sts)

ROUND 5: Join Color D, ch 5 (counts as 1 dc, ch 2), * skip 2 sts, dc in next st, (dc, ch 2, dc) in next st, dc in next st, ch 2, skip 2 sts, dc in next st, ch 1, skip next st **, dc in next st, ch 2; rep from * 4 more times, then from * to ** once, join to 3rd ch of beginning ch. (36 sts, 24 ch sp)

ROUND 6: Sl st into ch-2 sp, ch 3 (counts as 1 dc), 2 dc in same place, * 7 dc in corner ch-2 sp, 3 dc in next ch-2 sp, 2 dc in ch-1 sp **, 3 dc in next ch-2 sp; rep from * 4 more times, then from * to ** once, join to top of beginning ch. End Color D. (90 sts)

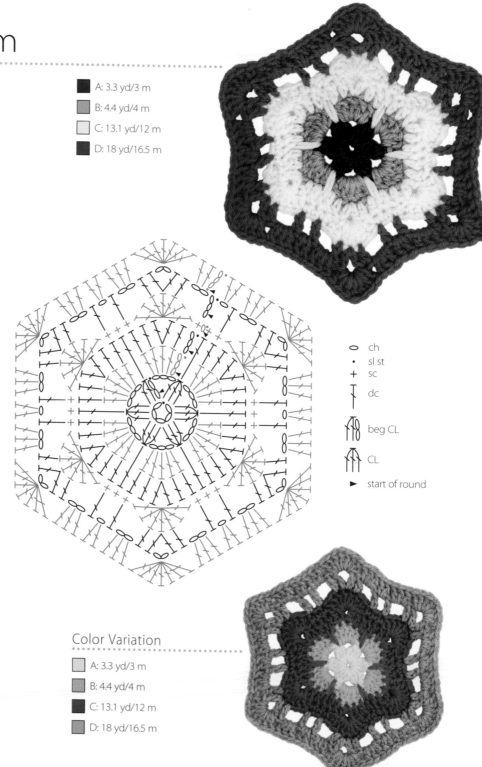

A: 3.3 yd/3 m
B: 4.4 yd/4 m
C: 13.1 yd/12 m
D: 18 yd/16.5 m

○	ch
•	sl st
+	sc
┬	dc
	beg CL
	CL
▶	start of round

Color Variation

A: 3.3 yd/3 m
B: 4.4 yd/4 m
C: 13.1 yd/12 m
D: 18 yd/16.5 m

Ipomoea

- **SKILL LEVEL:** Intermediate
- **SIZE OF HEXAGON:** 7 in. (18 cm)

■ A: 7.1 yd/6.5 m

■ B: 11 yd/10 m

■ C: 21.9 yd/20 m

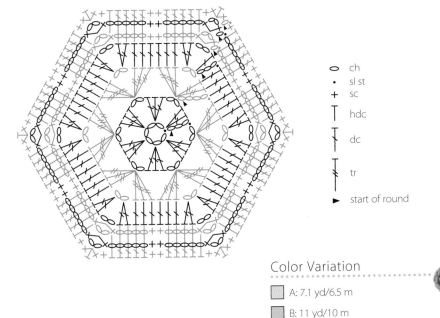

○ ch

• sl st

+ sc

T hdc

T dc

T tr

▶ start of round

Method

FOUNDATION RING: With Color A, ch 6 and join to form a ring.

ROUND 1: Ch 3 (counts as 1 dc), 2 dc into ring, [ch 2, 3 dc into ring] 5 times, ch 2, join to top of beginning ch. End Color A. (18 sts, 6 ch sp)

ROUND 2: Join Color B in next ch-2 sp, ch 4 (counts as 1 tr), (2 tr, ch 2, 3 tr) in same place, [(3 tr, ch 2 , 3 tr) in next ch-2 sp] 5 times, join to top of beginning ch. End Color B. (36 sts, 6 ch sp)

ROUND 3: Join Color C in next ch-2 sp, ch 3 (counts as 1 dc), (dc, ch 2, 2 dc) in same place, [dc in each st to next ch-2 sp, (2 dc, ch 2, 2 dc) in ch-2 sp] 5 times, dc in next 6 sts, join to top of beginning ch. End Color C. (60 sts, 6 ch sp)

ROUND 4: Join Color A in ch-2 sp, ch 1, [(sc, ch 2, sc) in ch-2 sp, ch 4, skip 4 sts, sc in next 2 sts, ch 4, skip 4 sts] 6 times, join to first sc made. End Color A. (24 sts, 18 ch sp)

ROUND 5: Join Color B in ch-2 sp, ch 1, [(sc, ch 2, sc) in ch-2 sp, ch 5, skip 1 st, sc in next 2 sts, ch 5, skip 1 st] 6 times, join to first sc made. End Color B. (24 sts, 18 ch sp)

ROUND 6: Join Color C in ch-2 sp, ch 1, [(sc, hdc, sc) in ch-2 sp, sc in next st; working behind ch of Rounds 4 and 5, hdc in next st of Round 4, dc in next 4 sts of Round 3, sc in next 2 sts of Round 5, dc in next 4 sts of Round 3, hdc in next st of Round 4, sc in next st of Round 5] 6 times, join to first sc made. End Color C. (102 sts)

Color Variation

■ A: 7.1 yd/6.5 m

■ B: 11 yd/10 m

■ C: 21.9 yd/20 m

Blume

- **SKILL LEVEL:** Intermediate
- **SIZE OF HEXAGON:** 7 in. (18 cm)

A: 1.6 yd/1.5 m
B: 2.2 yd/2 m
C: 7.7 yd/7 m
D: 11 yd/10 m
E: 6 yd/5.5 m
F: 9.8 yd/9 m

SPECIAL STITCHES:

Beg CL: Beginning cluster made of ch 5, dtr tbl in next 4 sts.
CL: Cluster made of dtr tbl in previous st and next 4 sts.

Method

FOUNDATION RING: With Color A, ch 4 and join to form a ring.

ROUND 1: Ch 3 (counts as 1 dc), 11 dc into ring, join to top of beginning ch. End Color A. (12 sts)

ROUND 2: Join Color B, ch 1, 2 sc in same place, 2 sc in next 11 sts, join to first sc made. End Color B. (24 sts)

ROUND 3: Join Color C tbl in previous sc, beg CL in same and next 4 sts, [ch 9, CL in same and next 4 sts] 5 times, ch 9, join to top of beg CL. End Color C. (6 CL, 6 ch sp)

ROUND 4: Join Color D in ch-9 sp, ch 1, 10 sc in each ch-9 sp around, join to first sc made. End Color D. (60 sts)

ROUND 5: Join Color E, ch 2 (counts as 1 hdc), * sc in next 8 sts, hdc in next st, (dc, ch 1, dc) into CL of Round 3 **, hdc in next st; rep from * 4 more times, then from * to ** once, join to top of beginning ch. End Color E. (72 sts, 6 ch sp)

ROUND 6: Join Color F, ch 3 (counts as 1 dc), [dc in each st to next corner ch-1 sp, (dc, ch 1, dc) in ch-1 sp] 6 times, dc in next st, join to top of beginning ch. End Color F. (84 sts)

ROUND 7: Join Color D in ch-1 sp, ch 1, [(sc, hdc, sc) in ch-1 sp, BPsc in each st to next corner ch-1 sp] 6 times, join to first sc made. End Color D. (102 sts)

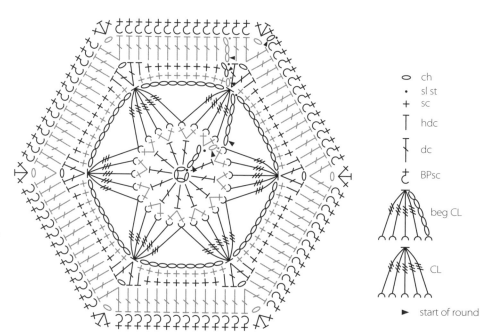

○ ch
• sl st
+ sc
T hdc
╪ dc
ᘐ BPsc

beg CL

CL

► start of round

Flor Bonita

- **SKILL LEVEL:** Intermediate
- **SIZE OF HEXAGON:** 7 in. (18 cm)

SPECIAL STITCHES:
Beg CL: Beginning cluster made of ch 3, 4 dc.
CL: Cluster made of 5 dc.

Method

FOUNDATION RING: With Color A, make a magic ring.

ROUND 1: Ch 3 (counts as 1 dc), 11 dc into ring, join to top of beginning ch. End Color A. (12 sts)

ROUND 2: Join Color B, ch 5 (counts as 1 dc, ch 2), (dc, ch 2) in next 11 sts, join to 3rd ch of beginning ch. End Color B. (12 sts, 12 ch sp)

ROUND 3: Join Color C in previous ch-2 sp, beg CL in same place, [ch 3, CL in next ch-2 sp] 11 times, ch 3, join to top of beg CL. End Color C. (12 CL, 12 ch sp)

ROUND 4: Join Color D, ch 1, 4 sc in each ch-3 sp around, join to first sc made. End Color D. (48 sts)

ROUND 5: Join Color E, ch 3 (counts as 1 dc), * 2 dc in next st, ch 3, 2 dc in next st, dc in next st, hdc in next st, sc in next 2 sts, hdc in next st **, dc in next st; rep from * 4 more times, then from * to ** once, join to top of beginning ch. End Color E. (60 sts, 6 ch sp)

ROUND 6: Join Color F, ch 1 and sc in same place, [sc in each st to corner ch-3 sp, (sc, hdc, sc) in ch-3 sp] 6 times, sc in next 7 sts, join to first sc made. End Color F. (78 sts)

ROUND 7: Join Color D, ch 3 (counts as 1 dc), [dc in each st to corner hdc, 3 dc in hdc] 6 times, dc in next 8 sts, join to top of beginning ch. End Color D. (90 sts)

A: 1.6 yd/1.5 m
B: 2.2 yd/2 m
C: 7.1 yd/6.5 m
D: 14.2 yd/13 m
E: 5.5 yd/5 m
F: 7.1 yd/6.5 m

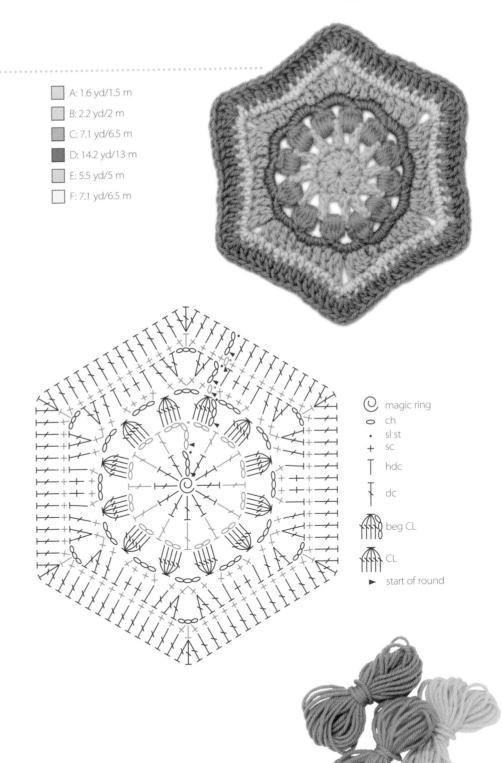

magic ring
ch
sl st
sc
hdc
dc
beg CL
CL
start of round

Skeleton Flower

- **SKILL LEVEL:** Intermediate
- **SIZE OF HEXAGON:** 7 in. (18 cm)

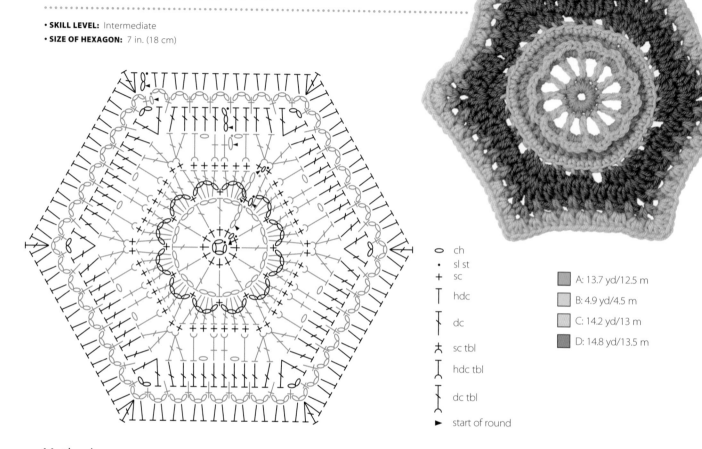

ⵔ	ch
•	sl st
+	sc
⊤	hdc
⊺	dc
ⵣ	sc tbl
ⵣ	hdc tbl
ⵣ	dc tbl
►	start of round

▦	A: 13.7 yd/12.5 m
▦	B: 4.9 yd/4.5 m
▦	C: 14.2 yd/13 m
▦	D: 14.8 yd/13.5 m

Method

FOUNDATION RING: With Color A, ch 4 and join to form a ring.

ROUND 1: Ch 1, 12 sc into ring, join to first sc made. End Color A. (12 sts)

ROUND 2: Join Color B, ch 5 (counts as 1 dc, ch 2), [dc in next st, ch 2] 11 times, join to 3rd ch of beginning ch. (12 sts, 12 ch sp)

ROUND 3: Ch 1 and sc in same, [ch 4, sc in next st] 11 times, ch 4, join to first sc made. End Color B. (12 sts, 12 ch sp)

ROUND 4: Hold ch 4 of previous round forward, join Color A in ch-2 sp of Round 2, ch 3 (counts as 1 dc), 3 dc in same place, [4 dc in next ch-2 sp of Round 2] 11 times, join to top of beginning ch. End Color A. (48 sts)

ROUND 5: Join Color C, ch 1 and sc in same place, sc in each st around, join to first sc made. End Color C. (48 sts)

ROUND 6: Join Color D tbl in 4th st to left of join, ch 1 and sc tbl in same place, * sc tbl in next st, ch 1, skip 1 st, hdc tbl in next st, [2 dc tbl in next st] twice, hdc tbl in next st, ch 1, skip 1 st **, sc tbl in next st; rep from * 4 more times, then from * to ** once, join to first sc made. (48 sts, 12 ch sp)

ROUND 7: Ch 3 (counts as 1 dc), dc in next st, * dc in ch-1 sp, dc in next 3 sts, (dc, ch 2, dc) in gap before next st, dc in next 3 sts, dc in ch-1 sp **, dc in next 2 sts; rep from * 4 more times, then from * to ** once, join to top of beginning ch. End Color D. (72 sts, 6 ch sp)

ROUND 8: Join Color A in next ch-2 sp, ch 1, * (sc, ch 3, sc) in ch-2 sp, ch 3, [sc in gap between next 2 sts, ch 3, skip 1 st] 6 times; rep from * 5 more times, join to first sc made. End Color A. (48 sts, 48 ch sp)

ROUND 9: Join Color C in next ch-3 sp, ch 2 (counts as 1 hdc), (hdc, dc, 2 hdc) in same place, * 2 hdc in each ch-3 sp to next corner ch-3 sp **, (2 hdc, dc, 2 hdc) in corner sp; rep from * 4 more times, then from * to ** once, join to top of beginning ch. End Color C. (114 sts)

Seedhead Skeleton

- **SKILL LEVEL:** Intermediate
- **SIZE OF HEXAGON:** 5 in. (13 cm)

Method

FOUNDATION RING: With Color A, ch 4 and join to form a ring.

ROUND 1: Ch 1, 12 sc into ring, join to first sc made. (12 sts)

ROUND 2: Working in front loop only, ch 7 (counts as 1 tr, ch 3), [tr tfl in next st, ch 3] 11 times, join to 4th ch of beginning ch. End Color A. (12 sts, 12 ch sp)

ROUND 3: Join Color B tbl of st on Round 1, ch 3 (counts as 1 dc), dc tbl in same place, 2 dc tbl in each st around, join to top of beginning ch. End Color B. (24 sts)

ROUND 4: Join Color C, ch 3 (counts as 1 dc), dc in same place, [dc in next st, 2 dc in next st] 11 times, dc in next st, join to top of beginning ch. (36 sts)

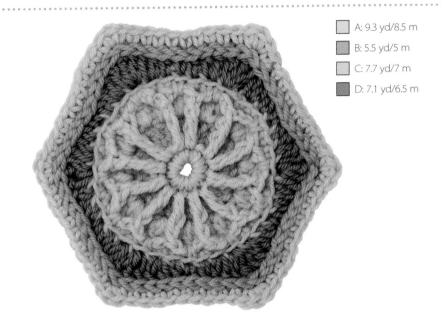

A: 9.3 yd/8.5 m
B: 5.5 yd/5 m
C: 7.7 yd/7 m
D: 7.1 yd/6.5 m

o	ch
•	sl st
+	sc
T	hdc
T	dc
T	tr
⊼	sc tbl
⊤	hdc tbl
⊤	dc tbl
⊤	tr tbl
⊤	tr tfl
▶	start of round

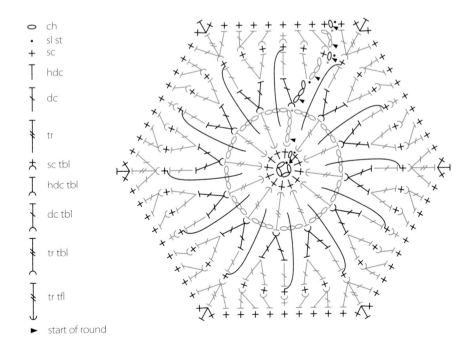

ROUND 5: Ch 1 and sc in same place, sc in next st, [sc in next st and into ch-3 sp of Round 2, sc in next 2 sts] 11 times, sc in next st and into ch-3 sp of Round 2, join to first sc made. End Color C. (36 sts)

ROUND 6: Join Color D tbl, ch 3 (counts as 1 dc), hdc tbl in same place, * hdc tbl in next st, sc tbl in next st, hdc tbl in next st, (hdc tbl, dc tbl) in next st, (dc tbl, tr tbl, dc tbl) in next st **, (dc tbl, hdc tbl) in next st; rep from * 4 more times, then from * to ** once, join to top of beginning ch. End Color D. (60 sts)

ROUND 7: Join Color A, ch 1 and sc in same place, [sc in each st to corner tr, (sc, hdc, sc) in tr] 6 times, sc in next st, join to first sc made. End Color A. (72 sts)

SURFACE CROCHET

With Color B, work slip stitches in the top of each st of Round 6.

Cluster of Grannies

- **SKILL LEVEL:** Intermediate
- **SIZE OF HEXAGON:** 7 in. (18 cm)

SPECIAL STITCHES:
Beg CL: Beginning cluster made of ch 3, 2 dc.
CL: Cluster made of 3 dc.

Method

FOUNDATION RING: With Color A, ch 6 and join to form a ring.

ROUND 1: Beg CL into ring, [ch 3, CL into ring] 5 times, ch 3, join to top of beg CL. End Color A. (6 CL, 6 ch sp)

ROUND 2: Join Color B in next ch-3 sp, (beg CL, ch 3, CL) in same place, [ch 2, (CL, ch 3, CL) in next ch-3 sp] 5 times, ch 2, join to top of beg CL. End Color B. (12 CL, 12 ch sp)

ROUND 3: Join Color C in next ch-3 sp, (beg CL, ch 3, CL) in same place, [ch 2, CL in ch-2 sp, ch 2, (CL, ch 3, CL) in next ch-3 sp] 5 times, ch 2, CL in next ch-2 sp, ch 2, join to top of beg CL. End Color C. (18 CL, 18 ch sp)

ROUND 4: Join Color D in next ch-3 sp, (beg CL, ch 3, CL) in same place, [(ch 2, CL in next ch-2 sp) twice, ch 2, (CL, ch 3, CL) in next ch-3 sp] 5 times, [ch 2, CL in next ch-2 sp] twice, ch 2, join to top of beg CL. End Color D. (24 CL, 24 ch sp)

ROUND 5: Join Color E in next ch-3 sp, (beg CL, ch 3, CL) in same place, [(ch 2, CL in next ch-2 sp) 3 times, ch 2, (CL, ch 3, CL) in next ch-3 sp] 5 times, [ch 2, CL in next ch-2 sp] 3 times, ch 2, join to top of beg CL. End Color E. (36 CL, 36 ch sp)

ROUND 6: Join Color F in next ch-3 sp, (beg CL, ch 3, CL) in same place, [(ch 2, CL in next ch-2 sp) 4 times, ch 2, (CL, ch 3, CL) in next ch-3 sp] 5 times, [ch 2, CL in next ch-2 sp] 4 times, ch 2, join to top of beg CL. End Color F. (42 CL, 42 ch sp)

A: 2.7 yd/2.5 m
B: 4.9 yd/4.5 m
C: 6.6 yd/6 m
D: 8.7 yd/8 m
E: 11 yd/10 m
F: 12.6 yd/11.5 m

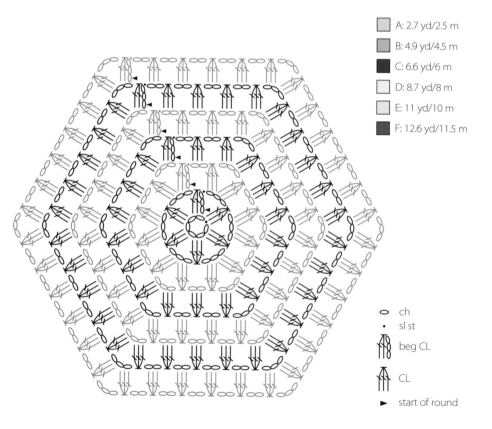

○ ch
• sl st
beg CL
CL
► start of round

Grandma's Motif

- **SKILL LEVEL:** Intermediate
- **SIZE OF HEXAGON:** 5 in. (13 cm)

A: 2.2 yd/2 m
B: 3.8 yd/3.5 m
C: 5.5 yd/5 m
D: 6 yd/5.5 m

SPECIAL STITCHES:
Beg CL: Beginning cluster made of ch 3, 1 dc.
CL: Cluster made of 2 dc.

Method

FOUNDATION RING: With Color A, ch 4 and join to form a ring.

ROUND 1: Beg CL into ring, [ch 3, CL into ring] 5 times, ch 3, join to top of beg CL. End Color A. (6 CL, 6 ch sp)

ROUND 2: Join Color B in next ch-3 sp, ch 3 (counts as 1 dc), 4 dc in same place, [5 dc in next ch-3 sp] 5 times, join to top of beginning ch. End Color B. (30 sts)

ROUND 3: Skip next st and join Color C in next st, ch 4 (counts as 1 dc, ch 1), dc in same place, [skip 2 sts, 5 dc in gap before next 5 dc group, skip 2 sts, (dc, ch 1, dc) in next st] 5 times, skip 2 sts, 5 dc in gap before next 5 dc group, join to 3rd ch of beginning ch. End Color C. (42 sts, 6 ch sp)

ROUND 4: Join Color D in next ch-1 sp, ch 4 (counts as 1 dc, ch 1), dc in same place, * ch 1, skip 1 st, dc in next 2 sts, hdc in next st, dc in next 2 sts ch 1, skip 1 st **, (dc, ch 1, dc) in next st; rep from * 4 more times, then from * to ** once, join to 3rd ch of beginning ch. End Color D. (42 sts, 18 ch sp)

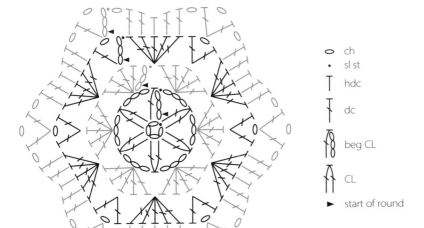

○	ch
•	sl st
T	hdc
⊤	dc
⋔	beg CL
⋀	CL
►	start of round

Seashore

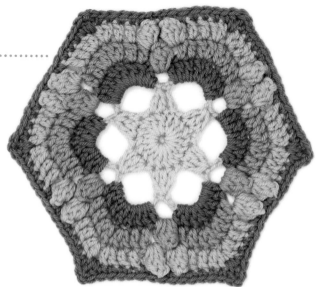

- **SKILL LEVEL:** Intermediate
- **SIZE OF HEXAGON:** 7 in. (18 cm)

A: 5.5 yd/5 m
B: 12.6 yd/11.5 m
C: 10.4 yd/9.5 m
D: 13.7 yd/12.5 m

SPECIAL STITCHES:
Beg CL: Beginning cluster made of ch 2, 2 dc.
CL: Cluster made of 3 dc.
PC: Popcorn made of 5 dc.

Method

FOUNDATION RING: With Color A, ch 5 and join to form a ring.

ROUND 1: Ch 3 (counts as 1 dc), 17 dc into ring, join to top of beginning ch. (18 sts)

ROUND 2: Beg CL over same and next 2 sts, [ch 7, CL over next 3 sts] 5 times, ch 7, join to top of beg CL. End Color A. (6 CL, 6 ch sp)

ROUND 3: Join Color B in next ch-7 sp, ch 3 (counts as 1 dc), 7 dc in same ch-7 sp, [8 dc in next ch-7 sp] 5 times, join to top of beginning ch. End Color B. (48 sts)

ROUND 4: Join Color C, sl st into next st, ch 3 (counts as 1 dc), dc in next st, * [2 dc in next st] twice, dc in next 2 sts, ch 1, skip 1 st, PC in space above CL of Round 2, ch 1, skip 1 st **, dc in next 2 sts; rep from * 4 more times, then from * to ** once, join to top of beginning ch. End Color C. (6 PC, 48 dc, 12 ch sp)

ROUND 5: Join Color D, sl st into next st, ch 3 (counts as 1 dc), dc in next st, * [2 dc in next st] twice, dc in next 2 sts, ch 1, skip 1 st, [PC in ch-1 sp, ch 1] twice, skip 1 st **, dc in next 2 sts; rep from * 4 more times, then from * to ** once, join to top of beginning ch. End Color D. (12 PC, 48 dc, 18 ch sp)

ROUND 6: Join Color B in corner sp between 2 sets of 2 dc, ch 4 (counts as 1 dc, ch 1), dc in same place, * sc in each st and ch sp to next space between corner sts **, (dc, ch 1, dc) in space between 2 sets of 2 dc; rep from * 4 more times, then from * to ** once, join to 3rd ch of beginning ch. End Color B. (90 sts, 6 ch sp)

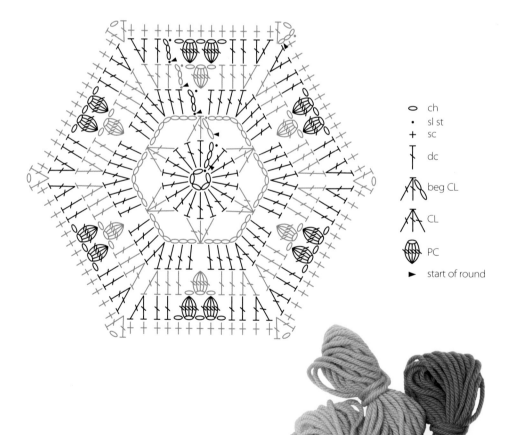

◯	ch
•	sl st
+	sc
⊤	dc
	beg CL
	CL
	PC
▶	start of round

Starfish

- **SKILL LEVEL:** Intermediate
- **SIZE OF HEXAGON:** 7 in. (18 cm)

SPECIAL STITCHES:

Beg PC: Beginning popcorn made of ch 3, 4 dc.

PC: Popcorn made of 5 dc.

Beg CL: Beginning cluster made of ch 2, 2 dc.

CL: Cluster made of 3 dc.

Method

FOUNDATION RING: With Color A, ch 5 and join to form a ring.

ROUND 1: Ch 3 (counts as 1 dc), 17 dc into ring, join to top of beginning ch. (18 sts)

ROUND 2: Beg CL over same and next 2 sts, [ch 6, CL over next 3 sts] 5 times, ch 6, join to top of beg CL. End Color A. (6 CL, 6 ch sp)

ROUND 3: Join Color B, beg PC in same place, * ch 2, (2 dc, 3 hdc, 2 dc) in ch-6 sp, ch 2 **, PC in next CL; rep from * 4 more times, then from * to ** once, join to top of beg PC. End Color B. (6 PC, 42 sts, 12 ch sp)

ROUND 4: Join Color C in previous ch-2 sp, beg PC in same place, * ch 5, skip PC, PC in next ch-2 sp, ch 1, skip 1 st, dc in next 5 sts, ch 1, skip 1 st **, PC in next ch-2 sp; rep from * 4 more times, then from * to ** once, join to top of beg PC. End Color C. (12 PC, 30 sts, 18 ch sp)

ROUND 5: Join Color D in next ch-5 sp, beg PC in same place, * ch 2, skip PC, dc in next ch-1 sp, dc in next 5 sts, dc in next ch-1 sp, ch 2 **, PC in next ch-5 sp; rep from * 4 more times, then from * to ** once, join to top of beg PC. End Color D. (6 PC, 42 sts, 12 ch sp)

ROUND 6: Join Color B, ch 1, [(sc, hdc, sc) in PC, 2 sc in next ch-2 sp, sc in next 7 sts, 2 sc in next ch-2 sp] 6 times, join to first sc made. End Color B. (84 sts)

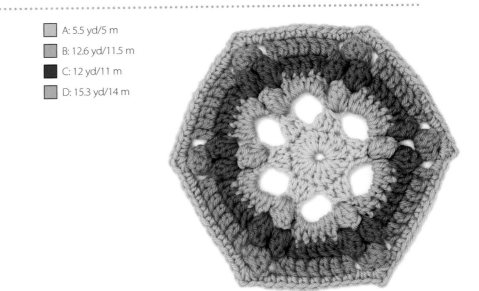

- ☐ A: 5.5 yd/5 m
- ☐ B: 12.6 yd/11.5 m
- ☐ C: 12 yd/11 m
- ☐ D: 15.3 yd/14 m

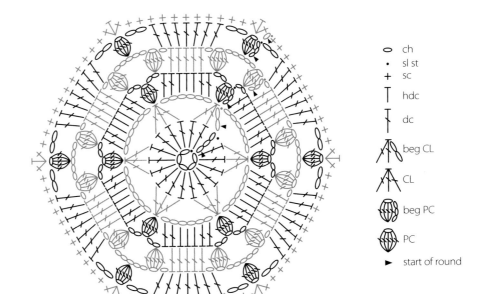

- o   ch
- •   sl st
- +   sc
- T   hdc
- ⊤   dc
- ⋀   beg CL
- ⋀   CL
- ⬢   beg PC
- ⬢   PC
- ►   start of round

Tessellate

- **SKILL LEVEL:** Intermediate
- **SIZE OF HEXAGON:** 7 in. (18 cm)

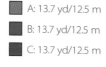

A: 13.7 yd/12.5 m
B: 13.7 yd/12.5 m
C: 13.7 yd/12.5 m

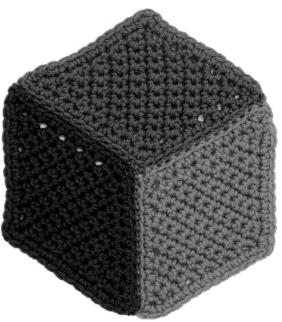

Method

DIAMONDS

Make 1 diamond in each color.

FOUNDATION ROW: Ch 2.

ROW 1: 2 sc in 2nd ch from hook, turn. (2 sts)

ROW 2: Ch 1, 2 sc in first st, sc in last st, turn. (3 sts)

ROW 3: Ch 1, 2 sc in first st, sc in each st to end, turn. (4 sts)

ROWS 4–11: Repeat Row 3. (12 sts)

ROW 12: Ch 1, sc2tog, sc in each st to end, turn. (11 sts)

ROWS 13–21: Repeat Row 12. (2 sts)

ROW 22: Ch 1, sc2tog. Do not end yarn.

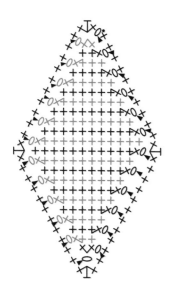

o   ch
•   sl st
+   sc
⊤   hdc
✕✕   sc2tog
►   start of row or round

EDGING EACH DIAMOND

Using same color, ch 1, (sc, hdc, sc) in top of sc2tog, sc in next 10 row edges, (sc, hdc, sc) in next row edge, sc in next 10 row edges, (sc, hdc, sc) in foundation ch, sc in next 10 row edges, (sc, hdc, sc) in next row edge, sc in next 10 row edges, join to first sc made. End Color A.

JOINING THE DIAMONDS

Using Color B, sew diamonds together through the back loops.

Diamond Flower

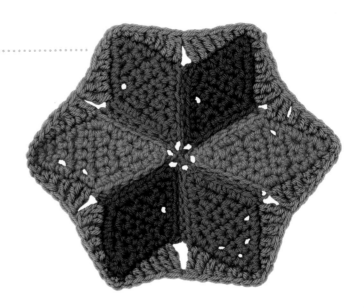

- **SKILL LEVEL:** Intermediate
- **SIZE OF HEXAGON:** 7 in. (18 cm)

A: 9.8 yd/9 m
B: 9.8 yd/9 m
C: 9.8 yd/9 m
D: 11 yd/10 m

Method

DIAMONDS
Make 2 diamonds each in Color A, Color B, and Color C.

FOUNDATION ROW: Ch 2.

ROW 1: 2 sc in 2nd ch from hook, turn. (2 sts)

ROW 2: Ch 1, 2 sc in first st, sc in last st, turn. (3 sts)

ROW 3: Ch 1, 2 sc in first st, sc in each st to end, turn. (4 sts)

ROWS 4–5: Repeat Row 3. (6 sts)

ROW 6: Ch 1, sc2tog, sc in each st to end, turn. (5 sts)

ROWS 7–9: Repeat Row 6. (2 sts)

ROW 10: Ch 1, sc2tog. Do not end yarn.

EDGING EACH DIAMOND
Using same color, ch 1, (sc, hdc, sc) in top of sc2tog, sc in next 4 row edges, (sc, hdc, sc) in next row edge, sc in next 4 row edges, (sc, hdc, sc) in foundation ch, sc in next 4 row edges, (sc, hdc, sc) in next row edge, sc in next 4 row edges, join to first sc made.

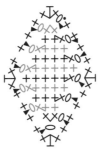

Single diamond with edging

o ch
• sl st
+ sc
⊤ hdc
† dc
⤬ sc2tog
⋔ tr2tog
► start of row or round

JOINING DIAMONDS INTO A FLOWER
Using Color B, sew diamonds together through the back loops.

EDGING THE FLOWER
Join Color D in hdc of any point, ch 1 and sc in same place, * ch 1, sc in next st, hdc in next st, dc in next 2 sts, [tr2tog] twice, dc in next 2 sts, hdc in next st, sc in next st, ch 1 **, sc in next hdc; rep from * 4 more times, then from * to ** once, join to first sc made. End Color D. (66 sts, 12 ch sp)

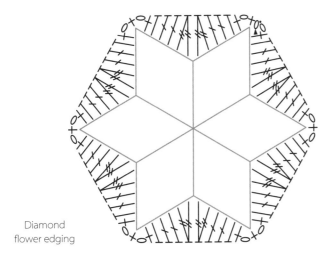

Diamond flower edging

Popcorn Corners

- **SKILL LEVEL:** Intermediate
- **SIZE OF HEXAGON:** 7 in. (18 cm)

SPECIAL STITCHES:
Beg PC: Beginning popcorn made of ch 3, 4 dc.
PC: Popcorn made of 5 dc.

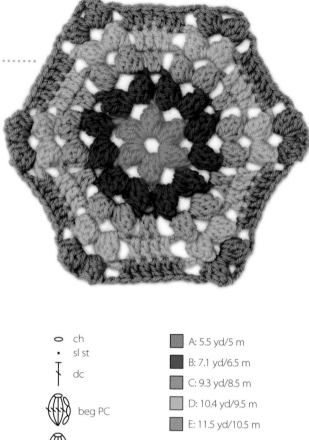

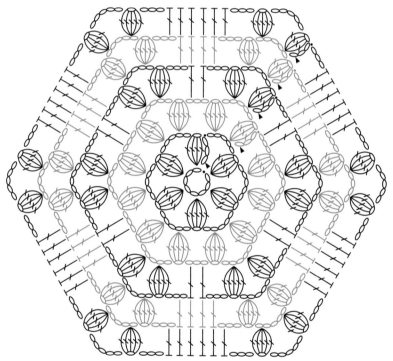

◯	ch
•	sl st
┬	dc
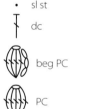	beg PC
	PC
►	start of round

▨	A: 5.5 yd/5 m
■	B: 7.1 yd/6.5 m
▨	C: 9.3 yd/8.5 m
▨	D: 10.4 yd/9.5 m
▨	E: 11.5 yd/10.5 m

Method

FOUNDATION RING: With Color A, ch 8 and join to form a ring.

ROUND 1: Beg PC into ring, [ch 5, PC into ring] 5 times, ch 5, join to top of beg PC. End Color A. (6 PC, 6 ch sp)

ROUND 2: Join Color B in previous ch-5 sp, (beg PC, ch 5, PC) in same place, [ch 3, (PC, ch 5, PC) in next ch-5 sp] 5 times, ch 3, join to top of beg PC. End Color B. (12 PC, 12 ch sp)

ROUND 3: Join Color C in next ch-5 sp, (beg PC, ch 5, PC) in same place, * ch 3, 2 dc in next ch-3 sp, ch 3 **, (PC, ch 5, PC) in next ch-5 sp; rep from * 4 more times, then from * to ** once, join to top of beg PC. End Color C. (12 PC, 12 dc, 18 ch sp)

ROUND 4: Join Color D in next ch-5 sp, (beg PC, ch 5, PC) in same place, * ch 3, dc in next ch-3 sp, dc in next 2 sts, dc in next ch-3 sp, ch 3 **, (PC, ch 5, PC) in next ch-5 sp; rep from * 4 more times, then from * to ** once, join to top of beg PC. End Color D. (12 PC, 24 dc, 18 ch sp)

ROUND 5: Join Color E in next ch-5 sp, (beg PC, ch 5, PC) in same place, * ch 3, dc in next ch-3 sp, dc in next 4 sts, dc in next ch-3 sp, ch 3 **, (PC, ch 5, PC) in next ch-5 sp; rep from * 4 more times, then from * to ** once, join to top of beg PC. End Color D. (12 PC, 36 dc, 18 ch sp)

Cluster Corners

- **SKILL LEVEL:** Intermediate
- **SIZE OF HEXAGON:** 7 in. (18 cm)

A: 4.9 yd/4.5 m
B: 6 yd/5.5 m
C: 8.2 yd/7.5 m
D: 9.3 yd/8.5 m
E: 11 yd/10 m

SPECIAL STITCHES:

Beg CL: Beginning cluster made of ch 2, 2 dc.
CL: Cluster made of 3 dc.

Method

FOUNDATION RING: With Color A, ch 8 and join to form a ring.

ROUND 1: Beg CL into ring, [ch 3, CL into ring] 11 times, ch 3, join to top of beg CL. End Color A. (12 CL, 12 ch sp)

ROUND 2: Join Color B in previous ch-3 sp, (beg CL, ch 3, CL) in same place, * ch 1, 2 dc in next ch-3 sp, ch 1 **, (CL, ch 3, CL) in next ch-3 sp; rep from * 4 more times, then from * to ** once, join to top of beg CL. End Color B. (12 CL, 12 dc, 18 ch sp)

ROUND 3: Join Color C in next ch-3 sp, (beg CL, ch 3, CL) in same place, * ch 1, dc in next ch-1 sp, dc in next 2 sts, dc in next ch-1 sp, ch 1 **, (CL, ch 3, CL) in next ch-3 sp; rep from * 4 more times, then from * to ** once, join to top of beg CL. End Color C. (12 CL, 24 dc, 18 ch sp)

ROUND 4: Join Color D in next ch-3 sp, (beg CL, ch 3, CL) in same place, * ch 1, dc in next ch-1 sp, dc in next 4 sts, dc in next ch-1 sp, ch 1 **, (CL, ch 3, CL) in next ch-3 sp; rep from * 4 more times, then from * to ** once, join to top of beg CL. End Color D. (12 CL, 36 dc, 18 ch sp)

ROUND 5: Join Color E in next ch-3 sp, (beg CL, ch 3, CL) in same place, * ch 1, dc in next ch-1 sp, dc in next 6 sts, dc in next ch-1 sp, ch 1 **, (CL, ch 3, CL) in next ch-3 sp; rep from * 4 more times, then from * to ** once, join to top of beg CL. End Color E. (12 CL, 48 dc, 18 ch sp)

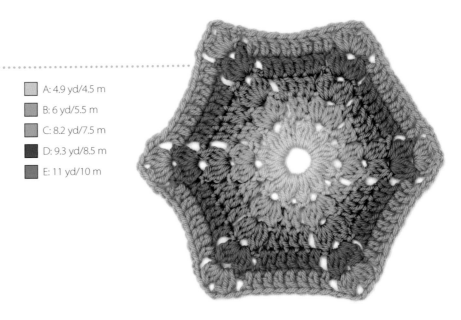

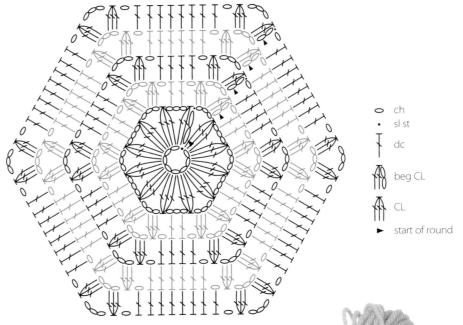

ch
sl st
dc
beg CL
CL
start of round

Bold Hexagon

- **SKILL LEVEL:** Intermediate
- **SIZE OF HEXAGON:** 7 in. (18 cm)

SPECIAL STITCH:

CL: Cluster made of 3 dc.

Method

FOUNDATION RING: With Color A, ch 8 and join to form a ring.

ROUND 1: Ch 4 (counts as 1 tr), [3 dc into ring, 1 tr into ring] 5 times, 3 dc into ring, join to top of beginning ch. End Color A. (24 sts)

ROUND 2: Join Color B, ch 5 (counts as 1 dc, ch 2), dc in same place, * ch 1, skip 1 st, CL in next st, ch 1, skip 1 st **, (dc, ch 2, dc) in next st; rep from * 4 more times, then from * to ** once, join to 3rd ch of beginning ch. End Color B. (6 CL, 12 dc, 18 ch sp)

ROUND 3: Join Color A, ch 1 and sc in same place, * (sc, hdc, sc) in next ch-2 sp, [sc in next st, sc into skipped st on Round 1] twice **, sc in next st; rep from * 4 more times, then from * to ** once, join to first sc made. End Color A. (48 sts)

ROUND 4: Join Color C, ch 1 and sc in same place, sc in next st, * (sc, ch 1, sc) in hdc **, sc in next 7 sts; rep from * 4 more times, then from * to ** once, sc in next 5 sts, join to first sc made. End Color C. (54 sts, 6 ch sp)

ROUND 5: Join Color B in ch-1 sp, ch 5 (counts as 1 dc, ch 2), dc in same place, * [ch 1, skip 1 st, CL in next st] 4 times, ch 1, skip 1 st **, (dc, ch 2, dc) in next ch-1 sp; rep from * 4 more times, then from * to ** once, join to 3rd ch of beginning ch. End Color B. (24 CL, 12 dc, 36 ch sp)

ROUND 6: Join Color C in ch-2 sp, ch 1, [(sc, hdc, sc) in ch-2 sp, (sc in next st, sc into skipped st of Round 4) 5 times, sc in next st] 6 times, join to first sc made. End Color C. (84 sts)

ROUND 7: Join Color D in corner hdc, ch 4 (counts as 1 dc, ch 1), dc in same place, [dc in next 13 sts, (dc, ch 1, dc) in next hdc] 5 times, dc in next 13 sts, join to 3rd ch of beginning ch. End Color D. (90 sts, 6 ch sp)

A: 8.2 yd/7.5 m
B: 14.2 yd/13 m
C: 11.5 yd/10.5 m
D: 11.5 yd/10.5 m

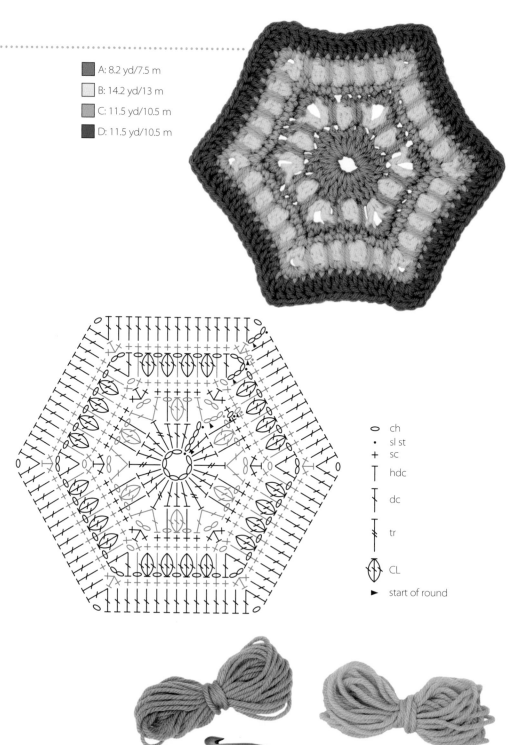

○ ch
• sl st
+ sc
T hdc
┬ dc
╪ tr
⬥ CL
► start of round

Bobble Hex

- **SKILL LEVEL:** Intermediate
- **SIZE OF HEXAGON:** 7 in. (18 cm)

■ A: 6.6 yd/6 m		■ D: 11 yd/10 m	
■ B: 6 yd/5.5 m		■ E: 11.5 yd/10.5 m	
■ C: 14.2 yd/13 m		■ F: 12 yd/11 m	

SPECIAL STITCH:
BO: Bobble made of 5 dc.

Method

FOUNDATION ROW: With Color A, ch 2.

ROW 1: 3 sc in 2nd ch from hook, turn. (3 sts)

ROW 2: Ch 1, 2 sc in first st, BO in next st, 2 sc in last st, turn. (5 sts)

ROW 3: Ch 1, 2 sc in first st, sc in next 3 sts, 2 sc in last st, turn. (7 sts)

ROW 4: Ch 1, 2 sc in first st, [sc in next st, BO in next st] twice, sc in next st, 2 sc in last st, turn. End Color A. (9 sts)

ROW 5: Join Color B, ch 1, 2 sc in first st, sc in each st to last, 2 sc in last st, turn. (11 sts)

ROW 6: Ch 1, 2 sc in first st, [sc in next st, BO in next st] 4 times, sc in next st, 2 sc in last st, turn. End Color B. (13 sts)

ROW 7: Join Color C and repeat Row 5. (15 sts)

ROW 8: Ch 1, 2 sc in first st, [sc in next st, BO in next st] 6 times, sc in next st, 2 sc in last st, turn. End Color C. (17 sts)

ROW 9: Join Color D and repeat Row 5. (19 sts)

ROW 10: Ch 1, 2 sc in first st, [sc in next st, BO in next st] 8 times, sc in next st, 2 sc in last st, turn. End Color D. (21 sts)

ROW 11: Join Color E, ch 1, sc in each st to end.

ROW 12: Ch 1, sc in next 2 sts, [BO in next st, sc in next st] 9 times, sc in last st, turn. End Color E.

ROW 13: Join Color F and repeat Row 11.

ROW 14: Ch 1, sc in next 3 sts, [BO in next st, sc in next st] 8 times, sc in next 2 sts, turn. End Color F.

ROWS 15–20: Repeat Rows 11 & 12 using Color C, then 13 & 14 using Color F, then 11 & 12 using Color E.

ROW 21: Join Color D, ch 1, sc2tog, sc in each st to last 2 sts, sc2tog, turn. (19 sts)

ROW 22: Ch 1, sc2tog, [BO in next st, sc in next st] 7 times, BO in next st, sc2tog, turn. End Color D. (17 sts)

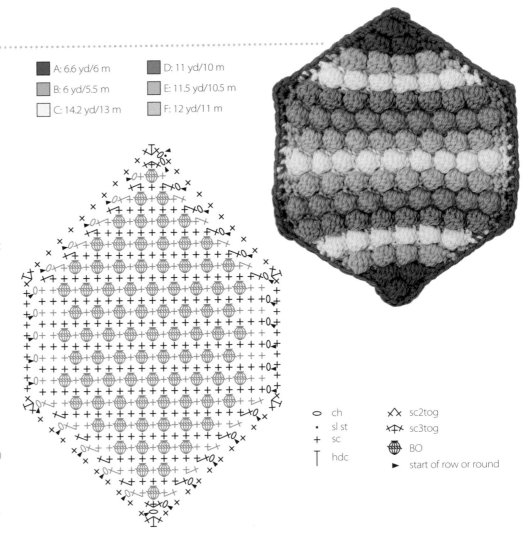

ROW 23: Join Color C and repeat Row 21. (15 sts)

ROW 24: Ch 1, sc2tog, [BO in next st, sc in next st] 5 times, BO in next st, sc2tog, turn. End Color C. (13 sts)

ROW 25: Join Color B and repeat Row 21. (11 sts)

ROW 26: Ch 1, sc2tog, [BO in next st, sc in next st] 3 times, BO in next st, sc2tog, turn. End Color B. (9 sts)

ROW 27: Join Color A and repeat Row 21. (7 sts)

ROW 28: Ch 1, sc2tog, BO in next st, sc in next st, BO in next st, sc2tog, turn. (5 sts)

ROW 29: Repeat Row 21. (3 sts)

ROW 30: Ch 1, sc in next st, BO in next st, sc in last st, turn. (3 sts)

ROW 31: Ch 1, sc3tog. End Color A. (1 st)

○	ch	✕	sc2tog
•	sl st	⋈	sc3tog
+	sc	⊕	BO
T	hdc	►	start of row or round

EDGING

Join Color A in same place, ch 1, (sc, hdc, sc) in same place, [sc in next 10 row edges, (sc, hdc, sc) in next row edge] twice, sc in next 10 row edges, (sc, hdc, sc) in foundation chain, [sc in next 10 row edges, (sc, hdc, sc) in next row edge] twice, sc in next 10 row edges, join to first sc made. End Color A.

PROJECT
Mix-and-Match Blanket

- **SKILL LEVEL:** Intermediate
- **SIZE OF HEXAGON:** 7 in. (18 cm)
- **FINISHED SIZE:** 34 x 58 in. (86 x 147 cm)
- **HOOK SIZE:** H (5 mm)
- **YARN WEIGHT:** DK/light worsted

SPECIAL STITCHES:
Beg CL: Beginning cluster made of ch 2, 2 dc.
CL: Cluster made of 3 dc.

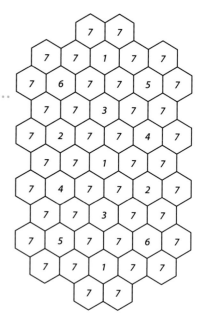

o	ch
•	sl st
+	sc
T	hdc
↑	dc
‡	sc thb
I	hdc thb
I	dc thb
⨍	BPtr
🗛	beg CL
🗛	CL
►	start of round

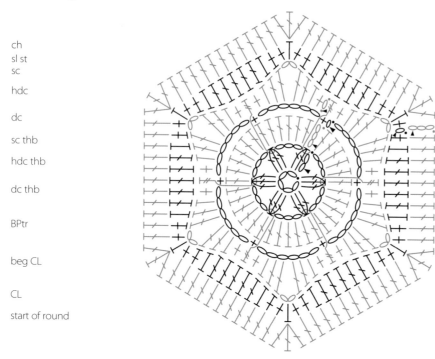

- A: 156.5 yd/143 m
- B: 67.5 yd/61.5 m
- C: 45 yd/41 m
- D: 45 yd/41 m
- E: 45 yd/41 m
- F: 45 yd/41 m
- G: 45 yd/41 m
- H: 1,072 yd/980 m

Method

HEXAGON 1 (MAKE 3)
FOUNDATION RING: With Color A, ch 5 and join to form a ring.
ROUND 1: Beg CL into ring, [ch 3, CL into ring] 5 times, ch 3, join to top of beg CL. End Color A. (6 CL, 6 ch sp)
ROUND 2: Join Color B, ch 3 (counts as 1 dc), [5 dc in ch-3 sp, dc in CL] 5 times, 5 dc in ch-5 sp, join to top of beginning ch. End Color B. (36 sts)
ROUND 3: Join Color A, ch 1 and sc in same place, [ch 6, skip 5 sts, sc in next st] 5 times, ch 6, skip 5 sts, join to first sc made. (6 sts, 6 ch sp)
ROUND 4: Sl st into ch-6 sp, ch 1, [(sc, hdc, 2 dc, ch 2, 2 dc, hdc, sc) in ch-6 sp, BPtr around CL of Round 1] 6 times, join to first sc made. End Color A. (54 sts, 6 ch sp)

ROUND 5: Join Color B in ch-2 sp, ch 1, [(sc, hdc, sc) in ch-2 sp, sc thb in next st, hdc thb in next st, dc thb in next 5 sts, hdc thb in next st, sc thb in next st] 6 times, join to first sc made. (72 sts)
ROUND 6: Ch 3 (counts as 1 dc), [3 dc in hdc, dc in next 11 sts] 5 times, 3 dc in next hdc, dc in next 10 sts, join to top of beginning ch. End Color B. (84 sts)

HEXAGONS 2–6 (MAKE 2 EACH)
HEXAGON 2: Use Color C instead of B.
HEXAGON 3: Use Color D instead of B.
HEXAGON 4: Use Color E instead of B.
HEXAGON 5: Use Color F instead of B.
HEXAGON 6: Use Color G instead of B.

HEXAGON 7 (MAKE 40)
With Color H, make 40 hexagons in the Windmill design (see page 38).

FINISHING
Following the layout diagram and using Color H, join the hexagons using slip stitch through the back loops.

PROJECT
Citrus Pillows

- **SKILL LEVEL:** Intermediate
- **SIZE OF HEXAGON:** 7 in. (18 cm)
- **FINISHED SIZE:** 14 in. (36 cm) square
- **HOOK SIZE:** J (5.5 mm)
- **YARN WEIGHT:** DK/light worsted
- **ADDITIONAL MATERIALS:** 14 in. (36 cm) square pillow form

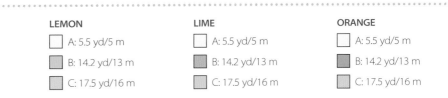

LEMON		LIME		ORANGE	
☐	A: 5.5 yd/5 m	☐	A: 5.5 yd/5 m	☐	A: 5.5 yd/5 m
☐	B: 14.2 yd/13 m	☐	B: 14.2 yd/13 m	☐	B: 14.2 yd/13 m
☐	C: 17.5 yd/16 m	☐	C: 17.5 yd/16 m	☐	C: 17.5 yd/16 m

Method

Make 8 hexagons per pillow in the colorway of your choice as follows:

FOUNDATION RING: With Color A, make a magic ring.

ROUND 1: Ch 1, 6 sc into ring, join to first sc made. End Color A. (6 sts)

ROUND 2: Join Color B tbl , ch 3 (counts as 1 dc), 2 dc tbl in same place, [3 dc tbl in next st] 5 times, join to top of beginning ch. (18 sts)

ROUND 3: Ch 3 (counts as 1 dc), dc in same place, [dc in next st, 2 dc in next st] 8 times, dc in next st, join to top of beginning ch. (27 sts)

ROUND 4: Ch 3 (counts as 1 dc), dc in next st, [2 dc in next st, dc in next 2 sts] 8 times, 2 dc in next st, join to top of beginning ch. End Color B. (36 sts)

ROUND 5: Join Color A, ch 1 and sc in same place, sc in next 2 sts, [trtr tfl of st on Round 1, sc in next 6 sts] 5 times, trtr tfl of st on Round 1, sc in next 3 sts, join to first sc made. End Color A. (42 sts)

ROUND 6: Join Color B thb, ch 1 and sc thb in same place, sc thb in next 2 sts, [2 sc thb in next st, sc thb in next 6 sts] 5 times, 2 sc thb in next st, sc thb in next 3 sts, join to first sc made. End Color B. (48 sts)

ROUND 7: Join Color C thb, ch 3 (counts as 1 dc), dc thb in same place, * dc thb in next st, hdc thb in next st, sc thb in next 2 sts, hdc thb in next st, dc thb in next st, 2 dc thb in next st, ch 1 **, 2 dc thb in next st; rep from * 4 more times, then from * to ** once, join to top of beginning ch. (60 sts, 6 ch sp)

ROUND 8: Ch 3 (counts as 1 dc), dc in same place, * dc in next 8 sts, 2 dc in next st, tr in ch-1 sp **, 2 dc in next st; rep from * 4 more times, then from * to ** once, join to top of beginning ch. (78 sts)

FINISHING

Following the layout diagram and using Color C, join the hexagons using slip stitch through the front loops, inserting the pillow form as you go.

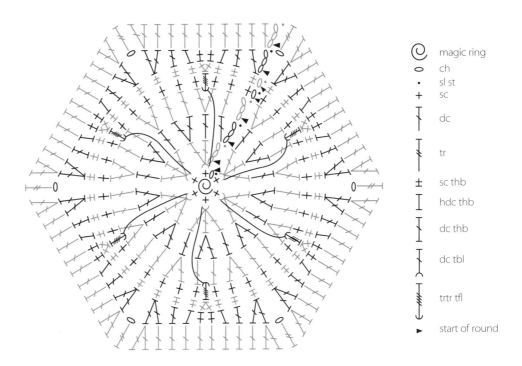

	magic ring
ᗡ	magic ring
ᴑ	ch
•	sl st
+	sc
⊤	dc
⊤	tr
±	sc thb
I	hdc thb
⊺	dc thb
⊺	dc tbl
⫯	trtr tfl
►	start of round

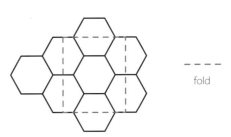

fold

Hanakotoba

- **SKILL LEVEL:** Advanced
- **SIZE OF HEXAGON:** 5 in. (13 cm)

SPECIAL STITCHES:
B7: Bullion stitch made with 7 wraps.
B9: Bullion stitch made with 9 wraps.

☐ A: 8.7 yd/8 m
■ B: 9.3 yd/8.5 m
▨ C: 11.5 yd/10.5 m
■ D: 6 yd/5.5 m

Method

FOUNDATION RING: With Color A, make a magic ring.

ROUND 1: Ch 1, 12 sc into ring, join to first sc made. (12 sts)

ROUND 2: Ch 3 (counts as 1 dc), dc in same place, 2 dc in next 11 sts, join to top of beginning ch. End Color A. (24 sts)

ROUND 3: Join Color B, [ch 2, B7 in same place, [ch 1, B9 in next st] twice, ch 1, B7 in next st, ch 2, sl st in same st, sl st in next st] 6 times. End Color B. (24 sts, 30 ch sp)

ROUND 4: Join Color C in sl st between petals, ch 3 (counts as 1 dc), 3 dc in same place, [ch 2, 3 dc in next sl st between petals] 5 times, ch 2, join to top of beginning ch. (24 sts, 6 ch sp)

ROUND 5: Ch 3 (counts as 1 dc), dc in same place, [dc in next 2 sts, 2 dc in next st, ch 1, 2 dc in next st] 5 times, dc in next 2 sts, 2 dc in next st, ch 1, join to top of beginning ch. End Color C. (36 sts, 6 ch sp)

ROUND 6: Join Color A, ch 1 and sc in same place, sc in next 5 sts, [2 hdc into space between two B9 of Round 3, sc in next 6 sts] 5 times, 2 hdc into space between two B9 of Round 3, join to first sc made. End Color A. (48 sts)

ROUND 7: With Color D, work standing BPdc in first st, * BPhdc in next st, BPsc in next 2 sts, BPhdc in next st, BPdc in next 2 sts, ch 2 **, BPdc in next 2 sts; rep from * 4 more times, then from * to ** once, BPdc in next st, join to top of standing BPdc. End Color D. (48 sts, 6 ch sp)

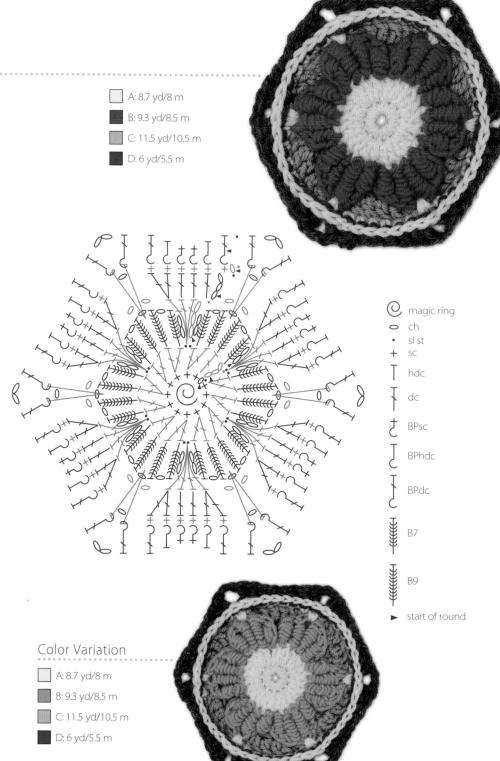

Color Variation

☐ A: 8.7 yd/8 m
▨ B: 9.3 yd/8.5 m
▨ C: 11.5 yd/10.5 m
■ D: 6 yd/5.5 m

◉ magic ring
◯ ch
• sl st
+ sc
T hdc
┬ dc
Ϛ BPsc
Ϟ BPhdc
Ϟ BPdc
⫯ B7
⫯ B9
► start of round

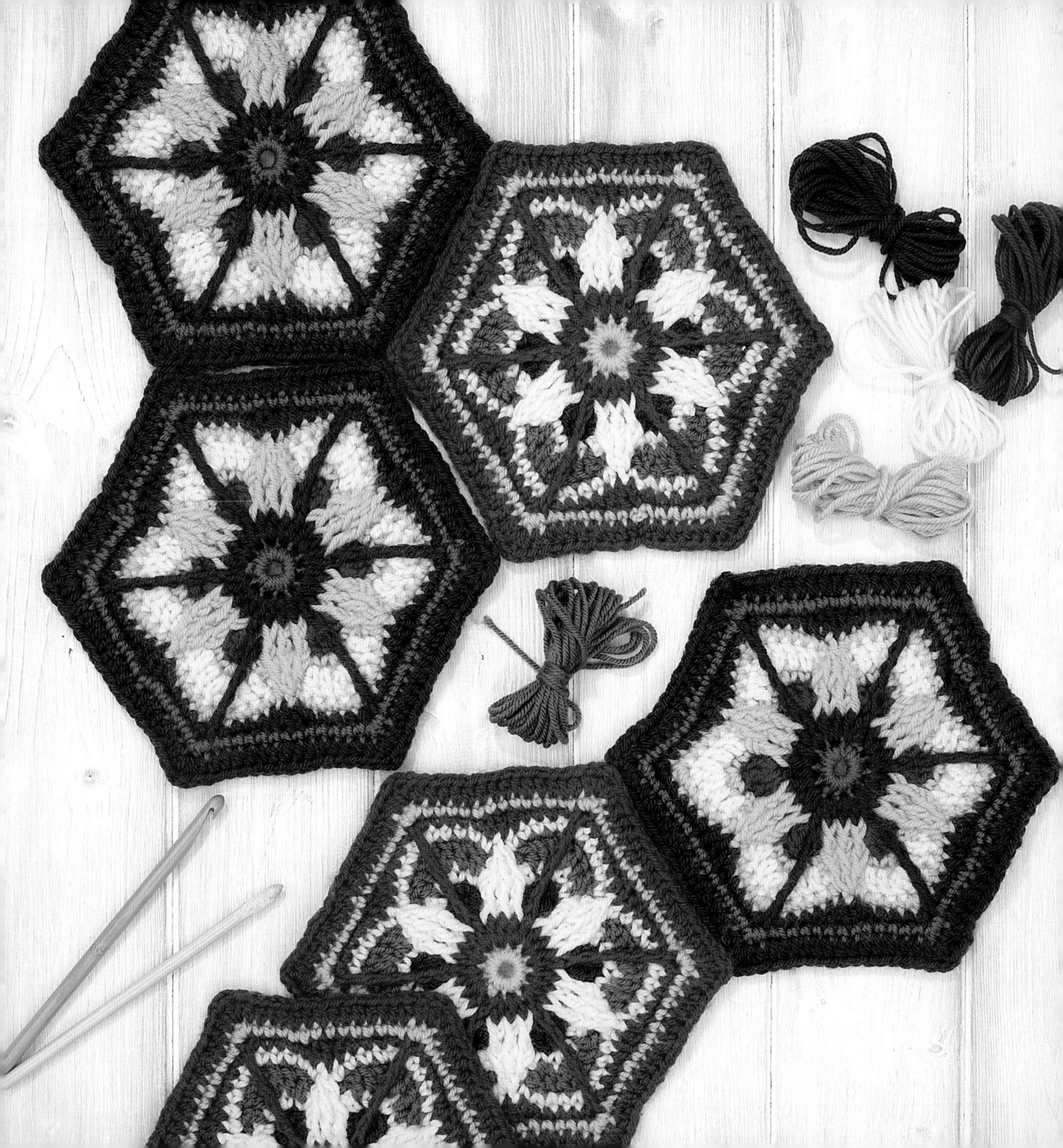

Chocolate Strawberries

- **SKILL LEVEL:** Advanced
- **SIZE OF HEXAGON:** 7 in. (18 cm)

SPECIAL STITCH:
CL: Cluster made of 3 FPdc worked over sts
2 rows below.

▨	A: 8.7 yd/8 m
▨	B: 11 yd/10 m
▨	C: 4.9 yd/4.5 m
▢	D: 12 yd/11 m
▨	E: 7.7 yd/7 m

Method

FOUNDATION RING: With Color A, ch 4 and
join to form a ring.
ROUND 1: Ch 1, 12 sc into ring, join to first sc
made. End Color A. (12 sts)
ROUND 2: Join Color B, ch 3 (counts as 1 dc),
dc in same place, 2 dc in next 11 sts, join to
top of beginning ch. End Color B. (24 sts)
ROUND 3: Join Color C, ch 3 (counts as 1 dc),
(tr, dc) in same place, [dc in next 3 sts, (dc, tr,
dc) in next st] 5 times, dc in next 3 sts, join to
top of beginning ch. End Color C. (36 sts)
ROUND 4: Join Color D, ch 1, [(sc, hdc, sc)
in next st, sc in next st, FPdc in next 3 sts
of Round 2, sc in next st] 6 times, join
to first sc made. End Color D. (48 sts)
ROUND 5: Join Color E, ch 3 (counts as
1 dc), [(dc, tr, dc) in next st, dc in next
7 sts] 5 times, (dc, tr, dc) in next st, dc
in next 6 sts, join to top of beginning ch.
End Color E. (60 sts)
ROUND 6: Join Color D in corner tr, ch 1,
[(sc, hdc, sc) in corner tr, sc in next 4 sts, skip
next st and CL into FPdc of Round 4, sc in
next 4 sts] 6 times, join to first sc made.
End Color D. (72 sts)
ROUND 7: Join Color B in corner hdc, ch 1, [(sc, FPtrtr
into dc of Round 2, sc) in corner hdc, sc in next 4 sts,
hdc in next st, dc in next st, hdc in next st, sc in next
4 sts] 6 times, join to first sc made. End Color B. (84 sts)
ROUND 8: Join Color A, ch 1 and sc in same place,
[(sc, hdc, sc) in next st, sc in next 13 sts] 5 times,
(sc, hdc, sc) in next st, sc in next 12 sts, join to first
sc made. End Color A. (96 sts)
ROUND 9: Join Color B, ch 2 (counts as 1 hdc), hdc in
next st, [(hdc, dc, hdc) in next st, hdc in next 15 sts]
5 times, (hdc, dc, hdc) in next st, hdc in next 13 sts,
join to top of beginning ch. End Color B. (108 sts)

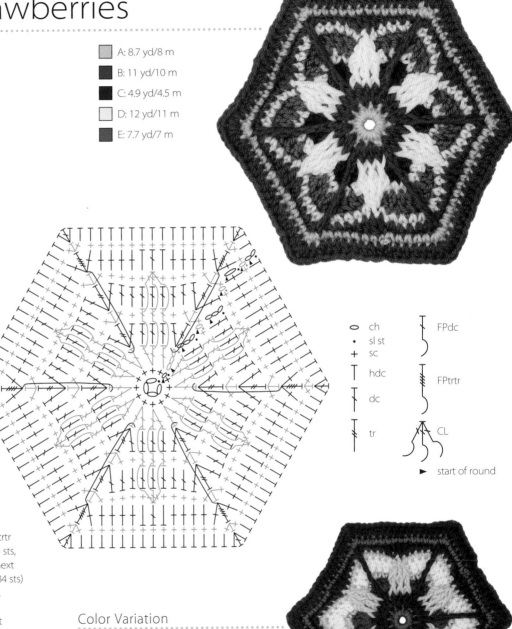

o	ch	⌐	FPdc
•	sl st		
+	sc	⌐	FPtrtr
⊤	hdc		
┼	dc	⌁	CL
╪	tr		
►	start of round		

Color Variation

▨	A: 8.7 yd/8 m	▨	D: 12 yd/11 m
▨	B: 11 yd/10 m	▨	E: 7.7 yd/7 m
▨	C: 4.9 yd/4.5 m		

Auricula

- **SKILL LEVEL:** Advanced
- **SIZE OF HEXAGON:** 5 or 7 in. (13 or 18 cm)

Method

FOUNDATION RING: With Color A, ch 5 and join to form a ring.

ROUND 1: Ch 3 (counts as 1 dc), [dc into ring, ch 2, dc into ring] 5 times, dc into ring, ch 2, join to top of beginning ch. End Color A. (12 sts, 6 ch sp)

5 in. (13 cm)

- A: 2.7 yd/2.5 m
- B: 3.8 yd/3.5 m
- C: 5.5 yd/5 m
- D: 7.1 yd/6.5 m

Color Variation

- A: 2.7 yd/2.5 m
- B: 3.8 yd/3.5 m
- C: 5.5 yd/5 m
- D: 7.1 yd/6.5 m

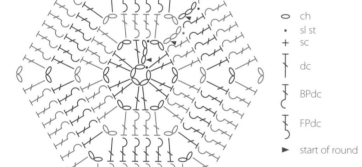

○ ch
• sl st
+ sc
╀ dc
╀ BPdc
╀ FPdc
► start of round

ROUND 2: Join Color B in ch-2 sp, ch 5 (counts as 1 dc, ch 2), dc in same place, * FPdc in next 2 sts, (dc, ch 2, dc) in ch-2 sp, BPdc in next 2 sts **, (dc, ch 2, dc) in ch-2 sp; rep from * once, then from * to ** once, join to 3rd ch of beginning ch. End Color B. (24 sts, 6 ch sp)

ROUND 3: Join Color C in ch-2 sp, ch 5 (counts as 1 dc, ch 2), dc in same place, * FPdc in each st to corner ch-2 sp, (dc, ch 2, dc) in ch-2 sp, BPdc in each st to corner ch-2 sp**, (dc, ch 2, dc) in ch-2 sp; rep from * once, then from * to ** once, join to 3rd ch of beginning ch. End Color C. (36 sts, 6 ch sp)

ROUND 4: Join Color D and repeat Round 3. End Color D. (48 sts, 6 ch sp)

TO MAKE 7 IN. (18 CM) HEXAGON

ROUND 5: Repeat Round 3 using Color E. (60 sts, 6 ch sp)

ROUND 6: Repeat Round 3 using Color F. (72 sts, 6 ch sp)

ROUND 7: Repeat Round 3 using Color G. (84 sts, 6 ch sp)

7 in. (18 cm)

- A: 2.7 yd/2.5 m
- B: 3.8 yd/3.5 m
- C: 5.5 yd/5 m
- D: 7.1 yd/6.5 m
- E: 8.7 yd/8 m
- F: 10.4 yd/9.5 m
- G: 11.5 yd/10.5 m

Frilly Flower

- **SKILL LEVEL:** Advanced
- **SIZE OF HEXAGON:** 7 in. (18 cm)

SPECIAL STITCH:
Spike sc: Worked over sts of previous round.

Method

FOUNDATION RING: With Color A, ch 4 and join to form a ring.

ROUND 1: Ch 1, 6 sc into ring, join to first st made. (6 sts)

ROUND 2: Ch 1, 12 spike sc into ring, join to first sc made. End Color A. (12 sts)

ROUND 3: Join Color B, ch 3 (counts as 1 dc), dc in same place, [2 dc in next st] 11 times, join to top of beginning ch. End Color B. (24 sts)

ROUND 4: Join Color C tfl, ch 5 (counts as 1 dtr), [dtr tfl in next st] 23 times, join to top of beginning ch. End Color C. (24 sts)

ROUND 5: Join Color B tbl, ch 1, [sc in next st and tbl of corresponding st on Round 3, ch 1] 24 times, join to first sc made. End Color B. (24 sts, 24 ch sp)

ROUND 6: Join Color A in ch-1 sp, ch 1 and sc in same place, sc in each ch-1 sp around, join to first sc made. (24 sts, 24 ch sp)

ROUND 7: Ch 1, 2 spike sc in each ch-1 sp of Round 5, join to first sc made. End Color A. (48 sts)

ROUND 8: Join Color D, ch 3 (counts as 1 dc), dc in same place, [dc in next st, 2 dc in next st] 23 times, dc in next st, join to top of beginning ch. End Color D. (72 sts)

ROUND 9: Join Color B in gap before next st, ch 1 and sc in same place, [ch 3, skip 3 sts, sc in gap before next st] 23 times, ch 3, join to first sc made. (24 sts, 24 ch sp)

ROUND 10: Sl st into ch-3 sp, ch 3 (counts as 1 dc), (dc, ch 2, 2 dc) in same place, * 3 hdc in next ch-3 sp, 3 sc in next ch sp, 3 hdc in next ch-3 sp **, (2 dc, ch 2, 2 dc) in next ch sp; rep from * 4 more times, then from * to ** once, join to top of beginning ch. End Color B. (78 sts, 6 ch sp)

☐	A: 9.3 yd/8.5 m
■	B: 18.6 yd/17 m
☐	C: 4.9 yd/4.5 m
☐	D: 9.3 yd/8.5 m

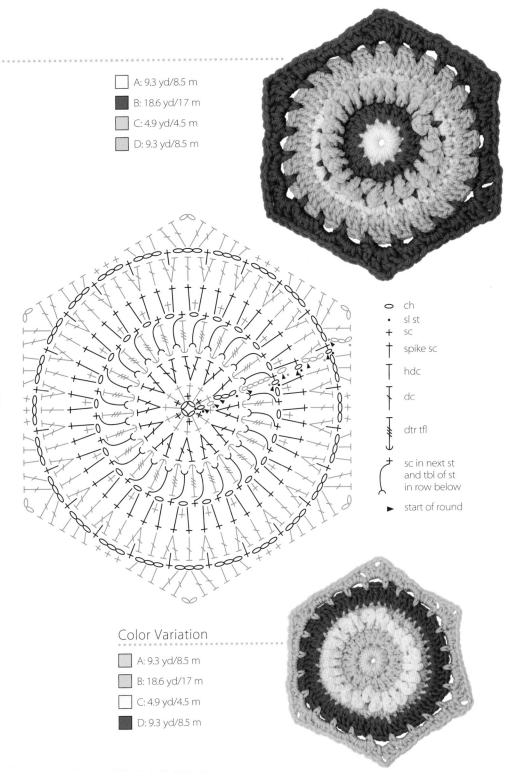

⬭	ch
•	sl st
+	sc
†	spike sc
T	hdc
⊤	dc
⫽	dtr tfl
⌣	sc in next st and tbl of st in row below
▶	start of round

Color Variation

☐	A: 9.3 yd/8.5 m
☐	B: 18.6 yd/17 m
☐	C: 4.9 yd/4.5 m
■	D: 9.3 yd/8.5 m

Starlight

- **SKILL LEVEL:** Advanced
- **SIZE OF HEXAGON:** 7 in. (18 cm)

□ A: 12.6 yd/11.5 m

▨ B: 20.8 yd/19 m

■ C: 12 yd/11 m

Method

STAR

FOUNDATION RING: With Color A, ch 4 and join to form a ring.

ROUND 1: Ch 3 (counts as 1 dc), 17 dc into ring, join to top of beginning ch. (18 sts)

ROUND 2: [Ch 7, sc in 2nd ch from hook, hdc in next 2 ch, dc in next 3 ch, skip 1 st of Round 1, (sl st in next st) twice] 6 times. End Color A. (6 star arms)

ᴑ	ch
•	sl st
+	sc
±	sc thb
Ⲧ	hdc
↑	dc
‡	dc thb
↟	dc tbl
►	start of round

Color Variation

▨ A: 20.2 yd/18.5 m

■ B: 13.1 yd/12 m

▨ C: 12 yd/11 m

HEXAGON

ROUND 1: Join Color B tbl of any unused st of Round 1 of the star, ch 3 (counts as 1 dc), 2 dc tbl in same place, [ch 2, 3 dc tbl in next empty st] 5 times, ch 2, join to top of beginning ch. (18 sts, 6 ch sp)

ROUND 2: Ch 3 (counts as 1 dc), dc in next 2 sts, [3 dc in ch-2 sp, dc in next 3 sts] 5 times, 3 dc in ch-2 sp, join to top of beginning ch. (36 sts)

ROUND 3: Ch 3 (counts as 1 dc), dc in next 3 sts, [3 dc in next st, dc in next 5 sts] 5 times, 3 dc in next st, dc in next st, join to top of beginning ch. End Color B. (48 sts)

ROUND 4: Join Color A, ch 1 and sc in same place, * sc in next st and into ch 1 at end of star arm, sc in next 3 sts, 3 sc in next st **, sc in next 3 sts; rep from * 4 more times, then from * to ** once more, sc in next 2 sts, join to first st made. End Color A. (60 sts)

ROUND 5: Join Color C thb of 2nd of previous 3 sc group, ch 3 (counts as 1 dc), 2 dc thb in same place, [dc thb in next 9 sts, 3 dc thb in next st] 5 times, dc thb in next 9 sts, join to top of beginning ch. End Color C. (72 sts)

ROUND 6: Join Color B thb, ch 1 and sc thb in same place, [3 sc thb in next st, sc thb in next 11 sts] 5 times, 3 sc thb in next st, sc thb in next 10 sts, join to first sc made. End Color B. (84 sts)

Checkers

- **SKILL LEVEL:** Advanced
- **SIZE OF HEXAGON:** 7 in. (18 cm)

Method

FOUNDATION RING: With Color A, ch 6 and join to form a ring.

ROUND 1: Ch 3 (counts as 1 dc), [dc into ring, ch 2, dc into ring] 5 times, dc into ring, ch 2, join to top of beginning ch. (12 sts, 6 ch sp)

ROUND 2: Sl st into ch-2 sp, ch 3 (counts as 1 dc), (dc, ch 2, 2 dc) in same place, * dc tbl in next 2 sts **, (2 dc, ch 2, 2 dc) in ch-2 sp; rep from * 4 more times, then from * to ** once, join to top of beginning ch. End Color A. (36 sts, 6 ch sp)

ROUND 3: Join Color B in ch-2 sp, ch 1, [(sc, hdc, sc) in ch-2 sp, sc tbl in next 2 sts, dc tfl in next 2 sts of Round 1, sc tbl in next 2 sts] 6 times, join to first sc made. End Color B. (54 sts)

ROUND 4: Join Color C tbl of hdc, ch 5 (counts as 1 dc, ch 2), dc tbl in same place, * dc tbl in next st, (dc tfl in next 2 sts, dc tbl in next 2 sts, dc tfl in next 2 sts) of Round 2, dc tbl in next st **, (dc tbl, ch 2, dc tbl) in next st; rep from * 4 more times, then from * to ** once, join to top of beginning ch. End Color C. (60 sts, 6 ch sp)

ROUND 5: Join Color D in ch-2 sp, ch 1, [(sc, hdc, sc) in ch-2 sp, (dc tfl in next 2 sts of Round 3, sc tbl in next 2 sts) twice, dc tfl in next 2 sts of Round 3] 6 times, join to first sc made. End Color D. (78 sts)

ROUND 6: Join Color E in next hdc, ch 5 (counts as 1 dc, ch 2), dc tbl in same place, * dc tbl in next st, [(dc tbl in next 2 sts, dc tfl in next 2 sts) of Round 4] twice, dc tbl in next 2 sts of Round 4, dc tbl in next st **, (dc tbl, ch 2, dc tbl) in next st; rep from * 4 more times, then from * to ** once, join to 3rd ch of beginning ch. End Color E. (84 sts, 6 ch sp)

ROUND 7: Join Color F in ch-2 sp, ch 1, [(sc, hdc, sc) in ch-2 sp, (sc in next 2 sts, dc tfl in next 2 sts of Round 5) 3 times, sc in next 2 sts] 6 times, join to first sc made. End Color F. (102 sts)

A: 7.1 yd/6.5 m
B: 4.9 yd/4.5 m
C: 8.2 yd/7.5 m
D: 7.7 yd/7 m
E: 10.4 yd/9.5 m
F: 11 yd/10 m

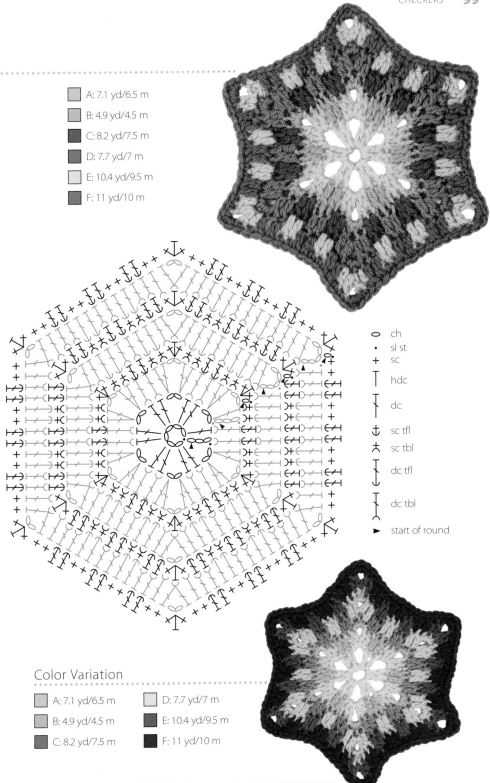

- ○ ch
- • sl st
- + sc
- ⊤ hdc
- ⊤ dc
- ⊥ sc tfl
- ⊁ sc tbl
- ⊤ dc tfl
- ⊤ dc tbl
- ► start of round

Color Variation

A: 7.1 yd/6.5 m	D: 7.7 yd/7 m
B: 4.9 yd/4.5 m	E: 10.4 yd/9.5 m
C: 8.2 yd/7.5 m	F: 11 yd/10 m

Ridges

- **SKILL LEVEL:** Advanced
- **SIZE OF HEXAGON:** 7 in. (18 cm)

A: 15.9 yd/14.5 m

B: 13.1 yd/12 m

C: 13.1 yd/12 m

D: 6.6 yd/6 m

Method

FOUNDATION RING: With Color A, ch 4 and join to form a ring.

ROUND 1: Ch 3 (counts as 1 dc), 11 dc into ring, join to top of beginning ch. End Color A. (12 sts)

ROUND 2: With Color B, work standing BPdc in first st of previous round, ch 2, BPdc in same st, [BPdc in next st, (BPdc, ch 2, BPdc) in next st] 5 times, BPdc in next st, join to top of standing BPdc. End Color B. (18 sts, 6 ch sp)

ROUND 3: Join Color C in ch-2 sp, ch 5 (counts as 1 dc, ch 2), dc in same place, * BPdc in next 3 sts **, (dc, ch 2, dc) in ch-2 sp; rep from * 4 more times, then from * to ** once, join to 3rd ch of beginning ch. End Color C. (30 sts, 6 ch sp)

ROUND 4: Join Color D in ch-2 sp, ch 5 (counts as 1 dc, ch 2), dc in same place, * BPdc in next 5 sts **, (dc, ch 2, dc) in ch-2 sp; rep from * 4 more times, then from * to ** once, join to 3rd ch of beginning ch. End Color D. (42 sts, 6 ch sp)

ROUND 5: Join Color C in ch-2 sp, ch 5 (counts as 1 dc, ch 2), dc in same place, * BPdc in next 7 sts **, (dc, ch 2, dc) in ch-2 sp; rep from * 4 more times, then from * to ** once, join to 3rd ch of beginning ch. End Color C. (54 sts, 6 ch sp)

ROUND 6: Join Color B in ch-2 sp, ch 5 (counts as 1 dc, ch 2), dc in same place, * BPdc in next 9 sts **, (dc, ch 2, dc) in ch-2 sp; rep from * 4 more times, then from * to ** once, join to 3rd ch of beginning ch. End Color B. (66 sts, 6 ch sp)

ROUND 7: Join Color A in ch-2 sp, ch 3 (counts as 1 dc), (dc, tr, 2 dc) in same place, * BPdc in next 11 sts **, (2 dc, tr, 2 dc) in ch-2 sp; rep from * 4 more times, then from * to ** once, join to top of beginning ch. End Color A. (96 sts)

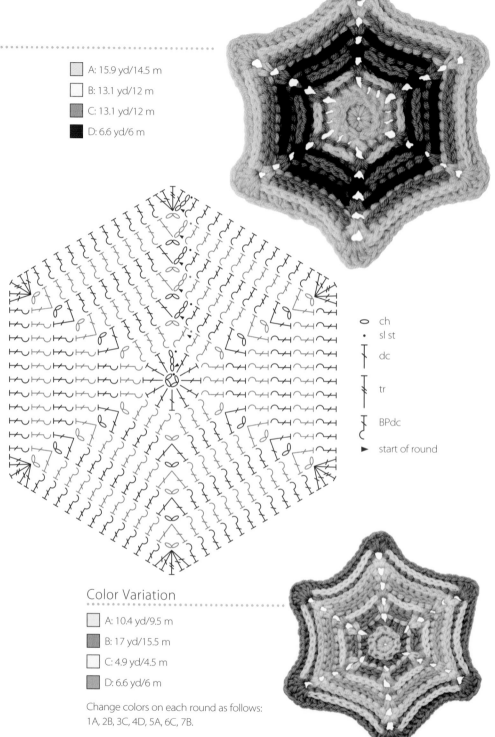

ch
sl st
dc
tr
BPdc
▶ start of round

Color Variation

A: 10.4 yd/9.5 m

B: 17 yd/15.5 m

C: 4.9 yd/4.5 m

D: 6.6 yd/6 m

Change colors on each round as follows:
1A, 2B, 3C, 4D, 5A, 6C, 7B.

Irish Rose

- **SKILL LEVEL:** Advanced
- **SIZE OF HEXAGON:** 5 in. (13 cm)

A:	3.3 yd/3 m
B:	5.5 yd/5 m
C:	15.9 yd/14.5 m
D:	13.1 yd/12 m

Method

FOUNDATION RING: With Color A, ch 4 and join to form a ring.

ROUND 1: Ch 3 (counts as 1 dc), 17 dc into ring, join to top of beginning ch. End Color A. (18 sts)

ROUND 2: Join Color B, ch 1 and sc in same place, [ch 3, skip 2 sts, sc in next st] 5 times, ch 3, join to first sc made. (6 sts, 6 ch sp)

ROUND 3: Sl st into ch-3 sp, ch 1, [(sc, hdc, 3 dc, hdc, sc) in ch-3 sp] 6 times, join to first sc made. End Color B. (42 sts)

ROUND 4: Join Color C in sc of Round 2 folding sts of last round forward and out of the way, ch 1 and sc in same place, [ch 4, sc in next sc of Round 2] 5 times, ch 4, join to first sc made. (6 sts, 6 ch sp)

ROUND 5: Sl st into ch-4 sp, ch 1, [(sc, hdc, 5 dc, hdc, sc) in ch-4 sp] 6 times, do not join. (54 sts)

ROUND 6: Sl st into sc of Round 4, ch 1 and sc in same place, [ch 5, sc in next sc of Round 4] 5 times, ch 5, join to first sc made. (6 sts, 6 ch sp)

ROUND 7: Sl st into ch-5 sp, ch 1, [(sc, hdc, 7 dc, hdc, sc) in ch-5 sp] 6 times, join to first sc made. End Color C. (66 sts)

ROUND 8: Join Color D in sc of Round 6, ch 1 and sc in same place, [ch 5, sc in next sc of Round 6] 5 times, ch 5, join to first sc made. (6 sts, 6 ch sp)

ROUND 9: Ch 5 (counts as 1 dc, ch 2), dc in same place, [6 dc in ch-5 sp, (dc, ch 2, dc) in next sc] 5 times, 6 dc in ch-5 sp, join to 3rd ch of beginning ch. (48 sts, 6 ch sp)

ROUND 10: Ch 1 and sc in same place, [3 sc in ch-2 sp, sc in next 8 sts] 5 times, 3 sc in ch-2 sp, sc in next 7 sts, join to first sc made. End Color D. (66 sts)

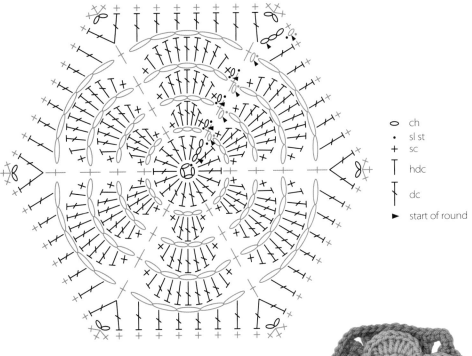

⟋	ch	
•	sl st	
+	sc	
⊤	hdc	
⊤	dc	
►	start of round	

Color Variation

A:	3.3 yd/3 m
B:	5.5 yd/5 m
C:	15.9 yd/14.5 m
D:	13.1 yd/12 m

Interlocking

- **SKILL LEVEL:** Advanced
- **SIZE OF HEXAGON:** 7 in. (18 cm)

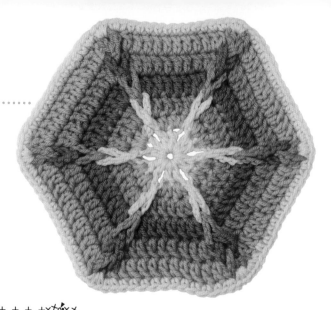

A: 11.5 yd/10.5 m
B: 12.6 yd/11.5 m
C: 16.4 yd/15 m
D: 8.7 yd/8 m

Method

FOUNDATION RING: With Color A, ch 4 and join to form a ring.

ROUND 1: Ch 3 (counts as 1 dc), [dc into ring, ch 10, dc into ring] 5 times, dc into ring, ch 10, join to top of beginning ch. End Color A. (12 sts, 6 ch sp)

ROUND 2: Join Color B, ch 2 (counts as 1 hdc), hdc in same place, [2 hdc in next st] 11 times, join to top of beginning ch. End Color B. (24 sts)

ROUND 3: Join Color C, ch 3 (counts as 1 dc), dc in same place, [dc in next 2 sts, 2 dc in next st, ch 10, 2 dc in next st] 5 times, dc in next 2 sts, 2 dc in next st, ch 10, join to top of beginning ch. End Color C. (36 sts, 6 ch sp) Twist ch 10 of Round 1 and pull ch 10 of Round 3 through from back to front.

ROUND 4: Join Color D, ch 3 (counts as 1 dc), dc in same place, [dc in next 4 sts, 2 dc in next st, ch 10, 2 dc in next st] 5 times, dc in next 4 sts, 2 dc in next st, ch 10, join to top of beginning ch. End Color D. (48 sts, 6 ch sp) Twist ch 10 of Round 3 and pull ch 10 of Round 4 through from back to front.

ROUND 5: Join Color C, ch 3 (counts as 1 dc), dc in same place, [dc in next 6 sts, 2 dc in next st, ch 10, 2 dc in next st] 5 times, dc in next 6 sts, 2 dc in next st, ch 10, join to top of beginning ch. End Color C. (60 sts, 6 ch sp) Twist ch 10 of Round 4 and pull ch 10 of Round 5 through from back to front.

ROUND 6: Join Color B, ch 3 (counts as 1 dc), dc in same place, [dc in next 8 sts, 2 dc in next st, ch 1, 2 dc in next st] 5 times, dc in next 8 sts, 2 dc in next st, ch 1, join to top of beginning ch. End Color B. (72 sts, 6 ch sp)

ROUND 7: Join Color A, ch 1 and 2 sc in same place, * sc in next 10 sts, 2 sc in next st, 3 sc in ch-1 sp and ch 10 of Round 5 making sure to twist the ch before working **, 2 sc in next st; rep from * 4 more times, then from * to ** once, join to first sc made. End Color A. (102 sts)

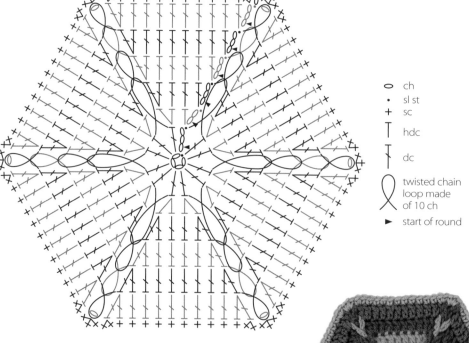

⊙	ch
•	sl st
+	sc
⊤	hdc
†	dc
⟨loop⟩	twisted chain loop made of 10 ch
►	start of round

Color Variation

A: 11.5 yd/10.5 m
B: 12.6 yd/11.5 m
C: 16.4 yd/15 m
D: 8.7 yd/8 m

Candy Swirl Flower

- **SKILL LEVEL:** Advanced
- **SIZE OF HEXAGON:** 5 in. (13 cm)

☐ A: 10.4 yd/9.5 m
■ B: 8.7 yd/8 m
▨ C: 16.4 yd/15 m

Method

FOUNDATION RING: With Color A, make a magic ring.

ROUND 1: Ch 1, 6 sc into ring, join to first sc made. End Color A. (6 sts)

ROUND 2: Join Color B thb, ch 1 and 2 sc thb in same place, [2 sc thb in next st] 5 times, join to first sc made. End Color B. (12 sts)

ROUND 3: Join Color A thb, ch 1 and 2 sc thb in same place, [sc tbh in next st, 2 sc thb in next st] 5 times, sc thb in next st, join to first sc made. End Color A. (18 sts)

ROUND 4: Join Color B thb, ch 1 and sc thb in same place, [sc thb in next st, 2 sc thb in next st, sc thb in next st] 5 times, sc thb in next st, 2 sc thb in next st, join to first sc made. End Color B. (24 sts)

ROUND 5: Join Color A thb, ch 1 and 2 sc thb in same place, [sc thb in next 3 sts, 2 sc thb in next st] 5 times, sc thb in next 3 sts, join to first sc made. (30 sts)

ROUND 6: Ch 1 and sc tfl in same place, ch 9, remove hook and join Color B in next st, ch 1 and sc tfl in same place, ch 9, [remove hook and pick up Color A, sc tfl in next st, ch 9, remove hook and pick up Color B, sc tfl in next st, ch 9] 14 times, join Color A to first sc worked in Color A, join Color B to first sc worked in Color B. End both colors. (30 sts, 30 ch sp)

ROUND 7: Join Color C tbl, ch 3 (counts as 1 dc), * (dc, tr, dc) tbl in next st **, dc tbl in next 4 sts; rep from * 4 more times, then from * to ** once, dc tbl in next 3 sts, join to top of beginning ch. (42 sts)

ROUND 8: Ch 3 (counts as 1 dc), dc in next st, * (dc, tr, dc) in next st **, dc in next 6 sts; rep from * 4 more times, then from * to ** once, dc in next 4 sts, join to top of beginning ch. (54 sts)

ROUND 9: Ch 1 and sc in same place, sc in next 2 sts, * 3 sc in next st **, sc in next 8 sts; rep from * 4 more times, then from * to ** once, sc in next 5 sts, join to first sc made. End Color C. (66 sts)

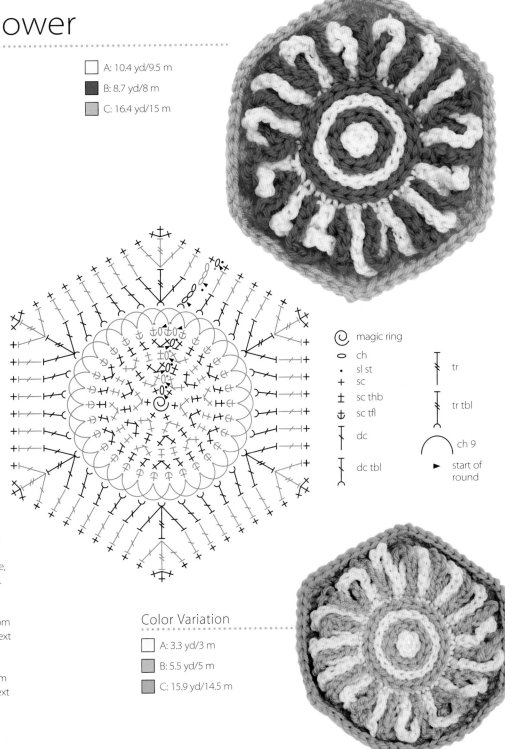

ⓒ magic ring
⊙ ch
• sl st
+ sc
‡ sc thb
⚓ sc tfl
│ dc
╽ dc tbl
╫ tr
╫╫ tr tbl
⌢ ch 9
► start of round

Color Variation

☐ A: 3.3 yd/3 m
▨ B: 5.5 yd/5 m
▨ C: 15.9 yd/14.5 m

Little Mill

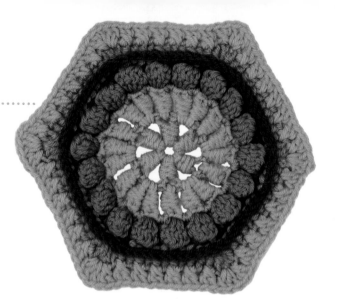

- **SKILL LEVEL:** Advanced
- **SIZE OF HEXAGON:** 7 in. (18 cm)

A: 6.6 yd/6 m
B: 21.3 yd/19.5 m
C: 13.1 yd/12 m
D: 8.2 yd/7.5 m
E: 7.7 yd/7 m

SPECIAL STITCHES:

Beg SCL: Beginning slanting cluster made of ch 3, [yo, insert hook under ch, yo and pull up loop] 3 times around ch, insert hook into ch sp or st, yo and pull through 6 loops on hook, yo and pull through remaining 2 loops on hook.

SCL: Slanting cluster made of dc in place indicated, [yo, insert hook under st, yo and pull up loop] 3 times around st, insert hook into next ch sp or st, yo and pull through 6 loops on hook, yo and pull through remaining 2 loops on hook.

CL: Cluster made of 4 tr in place indicated.

X st: Crossed stitch made of skip 1 st, dc in next st, dc in skipped st.

Method

FOUNDATION RING: With Color A, ch 4 and join to form a ring.

ROUND 1: Beg SCL, [ch 2, SCL] 5 times, ch 2, join to top of beg SCL. End Color A. (6 sts, 6 ch sp)

ROUND 2: Join Color B, beg SCL, ch 1, [(SCL, ch 1, SCL) in ch-2 sp, ch 1, SCL in next st, ch 1] 5 times, (SCL, ch 1, SCL) in next ch-2 sp, ch 1, join to top of beg SCL. End Color B. (18 sts, 18 ch sp)

ROUND 3: Join Color A in ch-1 sp, ch 1, 2 sc in each ch-1 sp, join to first sc made, turn. End Color A. (36 sts)

ROUND 4: Join Color C, ch 1 and sc in same place, sc in next st, [CL in gap before next st, sc in next 2 sts] 17 times, CL in space before next st, join to first sc made, turn. End Color C. (54 sts)

ROUND 5: Join Color D, ch 3 (counts as 1 dc), dc in same place, [skip CL, (2 dc in next sc) twice] 17 times, skip CL, 2 dc in next sc, join to top of beginning ch. End Color D. (72 sts)

ROUND 6: Join Color E in next CL of Round 4, ch 5 (counts as 1 tr, ch 1), tr in same place, [BPdc in next 12 sts, (tr, ch 1, tr) in CL of Round 4] 5 times, BPdc in next 12 sts, join to 4th ch of beginning ch. End Color E. (84 sts, 6 ch sp)

ROUND 7: Join Color B in ch-1 sp, ch 3 (counts as 1 dc), 2 dc in same place, [7 X st in next 14 sts, 3 dc in ch-1 sp] 5 times, 7 X st in next 14 sts, join to top of beginning ch. End Color B. (102 sts)

o   ch
•   sl st
+   sc
┬   dc
╫   tr
⌡   BPdc
         beg SCL
         SCL
         CL
X   X st

►   start of round
→   direction of work

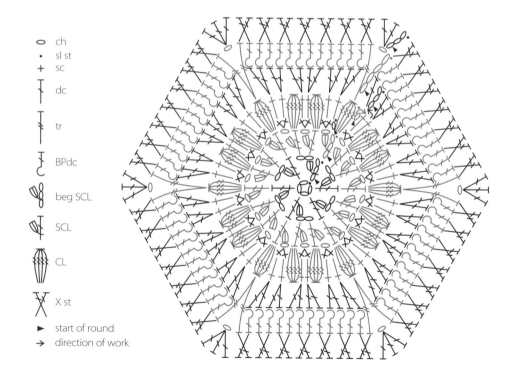

Felin Fach

- **SKILL LEVEL:** Advanced
- **SIZE OF HEXAGON:** 7 in. (18 cm)

■ A: 9.8 yd/9 m		□ E: 10.4 yd/9.5 m	
□ B: 12.6 yd/11.5 m		■ F: 6.6 yd/6 m	
■ C: 2.7 yd/2.5 m		□ G: 4.9 yd/4.5 m	
■ D: 8.7 yd/8 m		□ H: 13.1 yd/12 m	

SPECIAL STITCHES:

Beg PC: Beginning popcorn made of ch 3, 4 dc.
PC: Popcorn made of 5 dc.

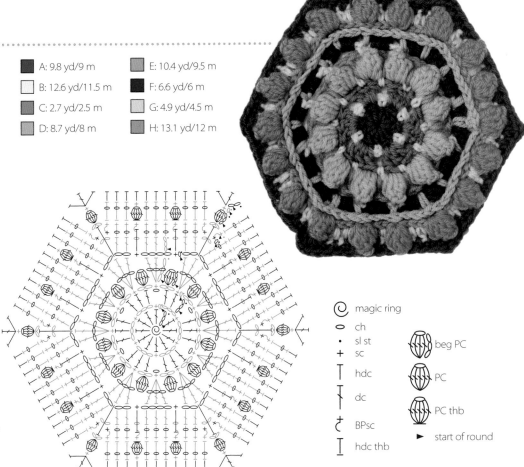

Method

FOUNDATION RING: With Color A, make a magic ring.

ROUND 1: Ch 3 (counts as 1 dc), 11 dc into ring, join to top of beginning ch. End Color A. (12 sts)

ROUND 2: Join Color B in next st, ch 1 and sc in same place, [ch 3, skip 1 st, sc in next st] 5 times, ch 3, join to first sc made. End Color B. (6 sts, 6 ch sp)

ROUND 3: Join Color C in previous ch sp, ch 3 (counts as 1 dc), 2 dc in same place, [ch 1, 3 dc in next ch sp] 5 times, ch 1, join to top of beginning ch. End Color C. (18 sts, 6 ch sp)

ROUND 4: Join Color B in next st, ch 1 and sc in same place, [ch 2, skip 1 st, sc in ch sp, ch 2, skip 1 st, sc in next st] 5 times, ch 2, skip 1 st, sc in ch sp, ch 2, join to first sc made. End Color B. (12 sts, 12 ch sp)

ROUND 5: Join Color D in next ch sp, beg PC, [ch 3, PC in next ch sp] 11 times, ch 3, join to top of first PC. End Color D. (12 sts, 12 ch sp)

ROUND 6: Join Color E in next sc of Round 4, ch 3 (counts as 1 dc), 2 dc in same place, [3 dc in next sc of Round 4] 11 times, join to top of beginning ch. End Color E. (36 sts)

ROUND 7: Join Color B in previous gap between dc groups, ch 1 and sc in same place, [ch 4, sc in gap between next dc groups] 11 times, ch 4, join to first sc made. End Color B. (12 sts, 12 ch sp)

ROUND 8: Join Color F in next ch sp, ch 3 (counts as 1 dc), 2 dc in same place, [ch 1, (2 dc, ch 2, 2 dc) in next ch sp, ch 1, 3 dc in next ch sp] 5 times, ch 1, (2 dc, ch 2, 2 dc) in next ch sp, ch 1, join to top of beginning ch. End Color F. (42 sts, 18 ch sp)

ROUND 9: Join Color G in previous corner ch sp, ch 1, [(sc, hdc in dc of Round 6, sc) in ch sp, ch 2, skip 2 sts, hdc in sc of Round 7, ch 3, skip 3 sts, hdc in sc of Round 7, ch 2, skip 2 sts] 6 times, join to first sc made. End Color G. (30 sts, 18 ch sp)

ROUND 10: With Color E, work standing BPsc in sc of previous round, ch 2, skip hdc, BPsc in next sc, * sc in next 2 dc of Round 8 behind ch sp, BPsc in next hdc, sc in next 3 dc of Round 8 behind ch sp, BPsc in next hdc, sc in next 2 dc of Round 8 behind ch sp **, BPsc in next sc, ch 2, skip hdc, BPsc in next sc; rep from * 4 more times, then from * to ** once, join to top of standing BPsc. End Color E. (66 sts, 6 ch sp)

ROUND 11: Join Color H in ch-2 sp, beg PC , * [ch 3, skip 3 sts, PC tbl in next BPsc] twice, ch 3, skip 3 sts **, PC in ch sp; rep from * 4 more times, then from * to ** once, join to top of beg PC. End Color G. (18 sts, 18 ch sp)

ROUND 12: Join Color B, ch 1 and sc in same place, * [working over ch-3 sp from previous round, hdc tbl in next 3 sts of Round 10, sc in PC] twice, hdc tbl in next 3 sts **, sc in PC; rep from * 4 more times, then from * to ** once, join to first sc made. End Color B. (72 sts)

ROUND 13: Join Color A, ch 2 (counts as 1 hdc), (dc, hdc) in same place, [hdc in next 11 sts, (hdc, dc, hdc) in next st] 5 times, hdc in next 11 sts, join to top of beginning ch. End Color A. (84 sts)

⟲ magic ring
○ ch
• sl st
+ sc
T hdc
🕇 dc
Ϛ BPsc
I hdc thb

🕸 beg PC
🕸 PC
🕸 PC thb
► start of round

Ridged Spokes

- **SKILL LEVEL:** Advanced
- **SIZE OF HEXAGON:** 7 in. (18 cm)

Method

FOUNDATION RING: With Color A, ch 4 and join to form a ring.

ROUND 1: Ch 1, 12 sc into ring, join to first sc made. End Color A. (12 sts)

ROUND 2: Join Color B tbl, ch 3 (counts as 1 dc), dc tbl in same place, 2 dc tbl in next 11 sts, join to top of beginning ch. End Color B. (24 sts)

ROUND 3: With Color C, work standing BPdc in same place, BPdc in next st, [tr tfl in next st on Round 1, BPdc in next 2 sts] 11 times, tr tfl in next st on Round 1, join to top of standing BPdc. End Color C. (36 sts)

ROUND 4: With Color D, work standing BPdc in same place, ch 1, [BPdc in next st, FPdc in next st, BPdc in next st, ch 1] 11 times, BPdc in next st, FPdc in next st, join to top of standing BPdc. End Color D. (36 sts, 12 ch sp)

ROUND 5: Join Color E in next ch-1 sp, ch 4 (counts as 1 dc, ch 1), dc in same place, * BPdc in next st, FPdc in next st, BPdc in next st, 2 dc in ch-1 sp, BPdc in next st, FPdc in next st, BPdc in next st **, (dc, ch 1, dc) in ch-1 sp; rep from * 4 more times, then from * to ** once, join to 3rd ch of beginning ch. End Color E. (60 sts, 6 ch sp)

ROUND 6: Join Color A in next ch-1 sp, ch 4 (counts as 1 dc, ch 1), dc in same place, * BPdc in next 2 sts, FPdc in next st, BPdc in next 4 sts, FPdc in next st, BPdc in next 2 sts **, (dc, ch 1, dc) in ch-1 sp; rep from * 4 more times, then from * to ** once, join to 3rd ch of beginning ch. End Color A. (72 sts, 6 ch sp)

ROUND 7: Join Color B in next ch-1 sp, ch 3 (counts as 1 dc), 2 dc in same place, * BPdc in next 3 sts, FPdc in next st, BPdc in next 4 sts, FPdc in next st, BPdc in next 3 sts **, 3 dc in ch-1 sp; rep from * 4 more times, then from * to ** once, join to top of beginning ch. End Color B. (90 sts)

ROUND 8: Join Color C, ch 3 (counts as 1 dc), 2 dc in same place, * [BPdc in next 4 sts, FPdc in next st] twice, BPdc in next 4 sts **, 3 dc in next st; rep from * 4 more times, then from * to ** once, join to top of beginning ch. End Color A. (102 sts)

▢	A: 8.7 yd/8 m
▢	B: 12 yd/11 m
▢	C: 15.9 yd/14.5 m
▢	D: 6 yd/5.5 m
▢	E: 7.1 yd/6.5 m

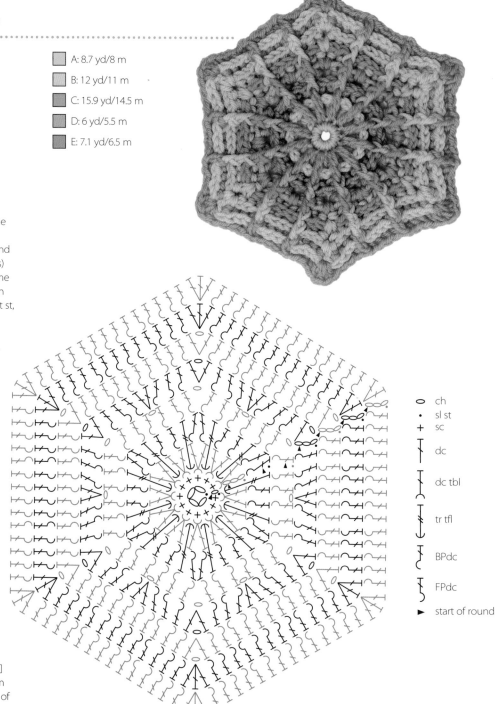

◯	ch
•	sl st
+	sc
⊥	dc
	dc tbl
	tr tfl
	BPdc
	FPdc
►	start of round

Smooth Spikes

- **SKILL LEVEL:** Advanced
- **SIZE OF HEXAGON:** 7 in. (18 cm)

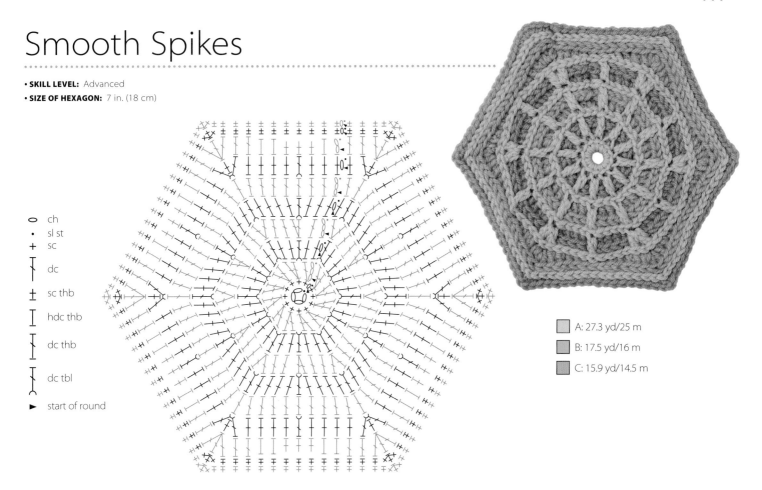

○	ch
•	sl st
+	sc
†	dc
±	sc thb
I	hdc thb
I	dc thb
ᛣ	dc tbl
►	start of round

A: 27.3 yd/25 m

B: 17.5 yd/16 m

C: 15.9 yd/14.5 m

Method

FOUNDATION RING: With Color A, ch 4 and join to form a ring.

ROUND 1: Ch 1, 12 sc into ring, join to first sc made. End Color A. (12 sts)

ROUND 2: Join Color B thb, ch 3 (counts as 1 dc), dc thb in same place, 2 dc thb in next 11 sts, join to top of beginning ch. End Color B. (24 sts)

ROUND 3: Join Color A thb, ch 1 and sc thb in same place, sc thb in next st, [dc tbl in sc of Round 1, sc thb in next 2 sts] 11 times, dc tbl in next sc of Round 1, join to first sc made. End Color A. (36 sts)

ROUND 4: Join Color C thb, ch 3 (counts as 1 dc), dc thb in next st, [2 dc thb in next st, dc thb in next 2 sts] 11 times, 2 dc thb in next st, join to top of beginning ch. End Color C. (48 sts)

ROUND 5: Join Color A thb, ch 1 and sc thb in same place, sc thb in next 2 sts, [dc tbl of dc of Round 3, sc thb in next 4 sts] 11 times, dc tbl in dc of Round 3, sc thb in next st, join to first sc made. End Color A. (60 sts)

ROUND 6: Join Color B thb, ch 3 (counts as 1 dc), dc thb in each st around, join to top of beginning ch. End Color B. (60 sts)

ROUND 7: Join Color A, ch 1 and sc thb in same place, sc thb in next 2 sts, * dc tbl in dc of Round 5, sc thb in next 4 sts, (dc tbl in dc of Round 5, sc in dc of previous round, dc tbl in dc on Round 5) in same place **, sc thb in next 4 sts; rep from * 4 more times, then from * to ** once, sc thb in next st, join to first sc made. End Color A. (72 sts)

ROUND 8: Join Color C thb, ch 2 (counts as 1 hdc), hdc thb in next st, * sc thb in next 3 sts, hdc tbh in next 2 sts, dc thb in next 2 sts, 3 dc thb in next st, dc thb in next 2 sts **, hdc thb in next 2 sts; rep from * 4 more times, then from * to ** once, join to top of beginning ch. End Color C. (84 sts)

ROUND 9: Join Color A thb, ch 1 and sc in same place, sc thb in next 9 sts, [3 sc thb in next st, sc thb in 13 sts] 5 times, 3 sc thb in next st, sc thb in next 3 sts, join to first sc made. End Color A. (96 sts)

ROUND 10: Join Color B thb, ch 1 and sc in same place, sc thb in next 10 sts, [3 sc thb in next st, sc thb in next 15 sts] 5 times, 3 sc thb in next st, sc thb in next 4 sts, join to first sc made. End Color B. (108 sts)

Flower Hex

- **SKILL LEVEL:** Advanced
- **SIZE OF HEXAGON:** 5 in. (13 cm)

SPECIAL STITCH:
B9: Bullion stitch made with 9 wraps.

Method

FOUNDATION RING: With Color A, ch 4 and join to form a ring.

ROUND 1: Ch 1, 12 sc into ring, join to first sc made. End Color A. (12 sts)

ROUND 2: Ch 3, [B9, ch 2] in 12 sts, join to top of first B9. End Color B. (12 sts, 12 ch sp)

ROUND 3: Join Color C in next ch-2 sp, ch 3 (counts as 1 dc), (dc, tr, ch 2, tr, 2 dc) in same place, [skip next ch-2 sp, (2 dc, tr, ch 2, tr, 2 dc) in next ch-2 sp] 5 times, skip next ch-2 sp, join to top of beginning ch. End Color C. (36 sts, 6 ch sp)

ROUND 4: Join Color D in previous skipped ch-2 sp, ch 3 (counts as 1 dc), (2 dc, ch 3, 3 dc) in same place, [(3 dc, ch 2, 3, dc) in next skipped ch-2 sp of Round 2] 5 times, join to top of beginning ch. (36 sts, 6 ch sp)

ROUND 5: Ch 3 (counts as 1 dc), dc in next 2 sts, [(2 dc, ch 2, 2 dc) in ch-3 sp, dc in next 6 sts] 5 times, (2 dc, ch 2, 2 dc) in next ch-3 sp, dc in next 3 sts, join to top of beginning ch. End Color D. (60 sts, 6 ch sp)

ROUND 6: Join Color A in next st, ch 1 and sc in same place, sc in next 3 sts, * 3 sc in ch-2 sp, sc in next 4 sts, [sc in next st and into ch-2 sp of Round 3] twice **, sc in next 4 sts; rep from * 4 more times, then from * to ** once, join to first sc made. End Color A. (76 sts)

A: 7.1 yd/6.5 m
B: 5.5 yd/5 m
C: 6 yd/5.5 m
D: 13.7 yd/12.5 m

○ ch
• sl st
+ sc
dc
tr
B9
► start of round

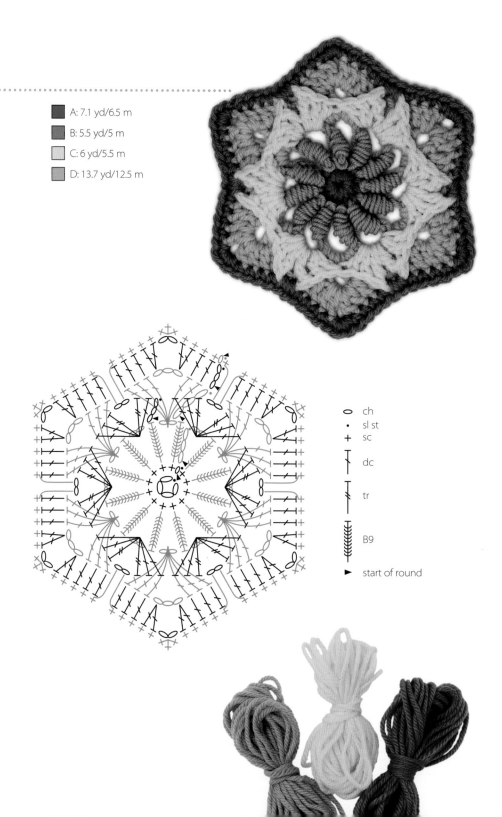

Ribbed Hex

- **SKILL LEVEL:** Advanced
- **SIZE OF HEXAGON:** 7 in. (18 cm)

A: 2.7 yd/2.5 m
B: 5.5 yd/5 m
C: 9.3 yd/8.5 m
D: 12.6 yd/11.5 m
E: 15.9 yd/14.5 m

Method

FOUNDATION RING: With Color A, ch 6 and join to form a ring.

ROUND 1: Ch 3 (counts as 1 dc), [dc into ring, ch 2 , dc into ring] 5 times, dc into ring, ch 2, join to top of beginning ch. End Color A. (12 sts, 6 ch sp)

ROUND 2: Join Color B in previous ch-2 sp, ch 3 (counts as 1 dc), (dc, ch 2, 2 dc) in same place, * FPdc in next 2 sts ** , (2 dc, ch 2 , 2 dc) in next ch-2 sp; rep from * 4 more times, then from * to ** once, join to top of beginning ch. End Color B. (36 sts, 6 ch sp)

ROUND 3: Join Color C in next ch-2 sp, ch 3 (counts as 1 dc), (dc, ch 2, 2 dc) in same place, * BPdc in next 2 sts, FPdc in next 2 sts, BPdc in next 2 sts ** , (2 dc, ch 2 , 2 dc) in next ch-2 sp; rep from * 4 more times, then from * to ** once, join to top of beginning ch. End Color C. (60 sts, 6 ch sp)

ROUND 4: Join Color D in next ch-2 sp, ch 3 (counts as 1 dc), (dc, ch 2, 2 dc) in same place, * [FPdc in next 2 sts, BPdc in next 2 sts] twice, FPdc in next 2 sts ** , (2 dc, ch 2 , 2 dc) in next ch-2 sp; rep from * 4 more times, then from * to ** once, join to top of beginning ch. End Color D. (84 sts, 6 ch sp)

ROUND 5: Join Color E in next ch-2 sp, ch 3 (counts as 1 dc), (dc, ch 2, 2 dc) in same place, * [BPdc in next 2 sts, FPdc in next 2 sts] 3 times, BPdc in next 2 sts ** , (2 dc, ch 2 , 2 dc) in next ch-2 sp; rep from * 4 more times, then from * to ** once, join to top of beginning ch. End Color E. (108 sts, 6 ch sp)

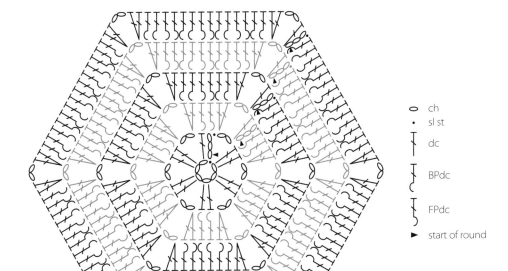

○ ch
• sl st
⊤ dc
╪ BPdc
╫ FPdc
► start of round

Sirius

- **SKILL LEVEL:** Advanced
- **SIZE OF HEXAGON:** 5 in. (13 cm)

Method

FOUNDATION RING: With Color A, make a magic ring.

ROUND 1: Ch 1, [sc into ring, ch 2] 6 times, join to first sc made. (6 sts, 6 ch sp)

ROUND 2: Ch 1, [2 sc in next st, ch 2] 6 times, join to first sc made. (12 sts, 6 ch sp)

ROUND 3: Ch 1, [sc in next st, sc2tog in last and next st, sc in same st, ch 2] 6 times, join to first sc made. (18 sts, 6 ch sp)

ROUND 4: Ch 1, [sc in next st, 2 sc in next st, sc in next st, ch 2] 6 times, join to first sc made. (24 sts, 6 ch sp)

ROUND 5: Ch 3 (counts as 1 dc), dc in same place, [dc in next 2 sts, 2 dc in next st, ch 2, skip ch-2 sp, 2 dc in next st] 5 times, dc in next 2 sts, 2 dc in next st, ch 2, join to top of beginning ch. (36 sts, 6 ch sp)

ROUND 6: Ch 3 (counts as 1 dc), dc in next 5 sts, [(2 dc, 1 tr, 2 dc) in ch-2 sp, dc in next 6 sts] 5 times, (2 dc, 1 tr, 2 dc) in ch-2 sp, join to top of beginning ch. End Color A. (66 sts)

SURFACE CROCHET

ROUND 1: Join Color B in ch-2 sp of Round 1, [(ch 2, dc, ch 2, dc, ch 2, sl st) in ch-2 sp, ch 1, sl st into next ch-2 sp] 6 times. End Color B.

ROUND 2: Join Color C in ch-2 sp of Round 2, [(ch 2, dc, ch 2, dc, ch 2, sl st) in ch-2 sp, ch 2, sl st into next ch-2 sp] 6 times. End Color C.

ROUND 3: Join Color D in ch-2 sp of Round 3, [(ch 2, dc ch 2, dc, ch 2, sl st) in ch-2 sp, ch 3, sl st into next ch-2 sp] 6 times. End Color D.

ROUND 4: Join Color E in ch-2 sp of Round 4, [(ch 2, dc, ch 2, dc, ch 2, sl st) in ch-2 sp, ch 4, sl st into next ch-2 sp] 6 times. End Color E.

A: 18.6 yd/17 m
B: 4.4 yd/4 m
C: 4.4 yd/4 m
D: 4.4 yd/4 m
E: 4.4 yd/4 m

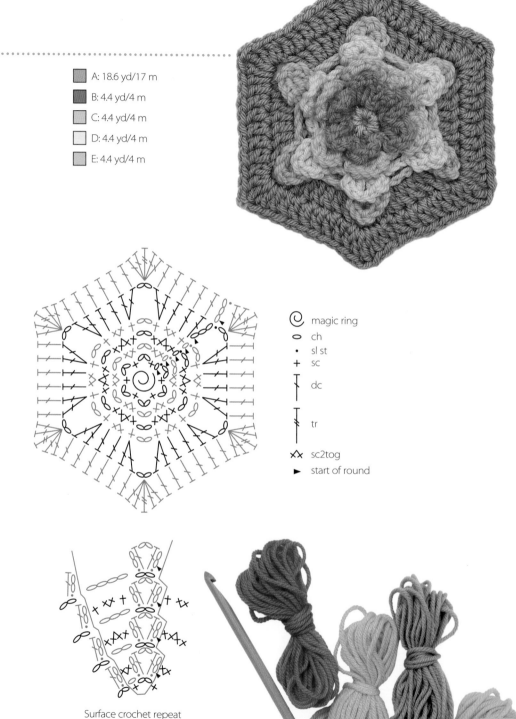

⟲ magic ring
◯ ch
• sl st
+ sc
│ dc
╪ tr
⤬ sc2tog
► start of round

Surface crochet repeat

Marigold

- **SKILL LEVEL:** Advanced
- **SIZE OF HEXAGON:** 7 in. (18 cm)

A: 12 yd/11 m
B: 8.7 yd/8 m
C: 6.6 yd/6 m
D: 8.2 yd/7.5 m
E: 23.5 yd/21.5 m

Method

FOUNDATION RING: With Color A, make a magic ring.
ROUND 1: Ch 1, 9 sc into ring, join to first sc made. End Color A. (9 sts)
ROUND 2: Join Color B, ch 1, 2 sc in each st around, join to first sc made. End Color B. (18 sts)
ROUND 3: Join Color C, ch 1 and sc in same place, [ch 3, skip 2 sts, sc in next st] 5 times, ch 3, join to first sc made. (6 sts, 6 ch sp)
ROUND 4: Sl st into ch-3 sp, ch 1, (sc, ch 3, 5 dc, ch 3, sc) in each ch-3 sp around, join to first sc made. End Color C. (6 petals)
ROUND 5: Join Color D in gap between 2 sc, ch 1 and sc in same place, [ch 4, sc in gap between next 2 sc] 5 times, ch 4, join to first sc made. (6 sts, 6 ch sp)
ROUND 6: Sl st into ch-4 sp, ch 1, (sc, ch 3, 7 dc, ch 3, sc) in each ch-4 sp around, join to first sc made. End Color D. (6 petals)
ROUND 7: Join Color E in gap between 2 sc, ch 1 and sc in same place, [ch 5, sc in gap between next 2 sc] 5 times, ch 5, join to first sc made. (6 sts, 6 ch sp)
ROUND 8: Sl st into ch-5 sp, ch 1, (sc, ch 3, 9 dc, ch 3, sc) in each ch-5 sp around, join to first sc made. End Color E. (6 petals)
ROUND 9: Join Color A in gap between 2 sc, ch 1 and sc in same place, [ch 6, sc in gap between next 2 sc] 5 times, ch 6, join to first sc made. (6 sts, 6 ch sp)
ROUND 10: Ch 5 (counts as 1 dc, ch 2), dc in same place, [8 dc in next ch-6 sp, (dc, ch 2, dc) in sc] 5 times, 8 dc in next ch-6 sp, join to top of beginning ch. (60 sts, 6 ch sp)
ROUND 11: Ch 3 (counts as 1 dc), [(dc, ch 2, dc) in next ch-2 sp, dc in next 10 sts] 5 times, (dc, ch 2, dc) in next ch-2 sp, dc in next 9 sts, join to top of beginning ch. End Color A. (72 sts, 6 ch sp)
ROUND 12: Join Color B, ch 1 and sc in same place, sc in next st, [(sc, ch 1, sc) in next ch-2 sp, sc in next 12 sts] 5 times, (sc, ch 1, sc) in next ch-2 sp, sc in next 10 sts, join to first sc made. End Color B. (84 sts, 6 ch sp)

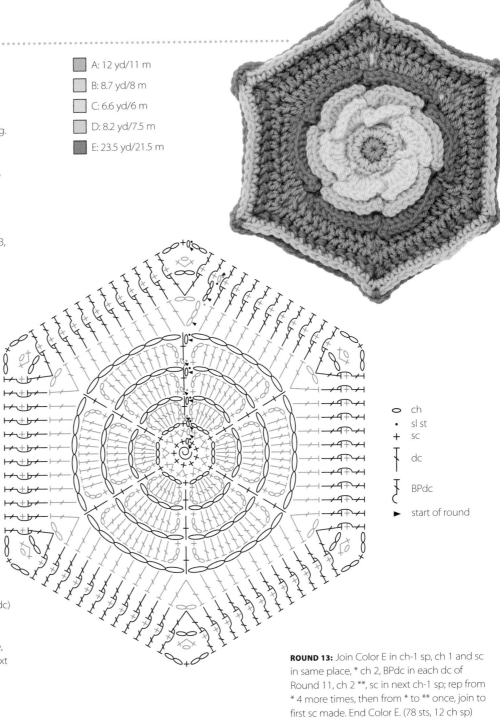

o ch
· sl st
+ sc
dc
BPdc
► start of round

ROUND 13: Join Color E in ch-1 sp, ch 1 and sc in same place, * ch 2, BPdc in each dc of Round 11, ch 2 **, sc in next ch-1 sp; rep from * 4 more times, then from * to ** once, join to first sc made. End Color E. (78 sts, 12 ch sp)

Rosa Canina

• **SKILL LEVEL:** Advanced
• **SIZE OF HEXAGON:** 7 in. (18 cm)

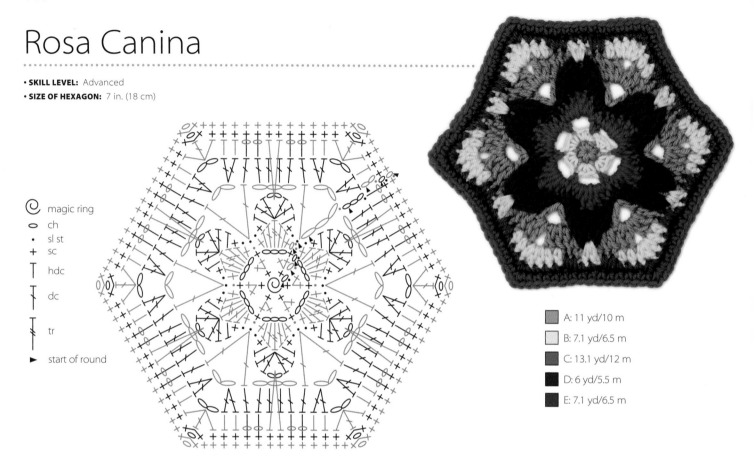

magic ring
ch
sl st
sc
hdc
dc
tr
► start of round

A: 11 yd/10 m
B: 7.1 yd/6.5 m
C: 13.1 yd/12 m
D: 6 yd/5.5 m
E: 7.1 yd/6.5 m

Method

FOUNDATION RING: With Color A, make a magic ring.

ROUND 1: Ch 1, 6 sc into ring, join to first sc made. End Color A. (6 sts)

ROUND 2: Join Color B, ch 1, 2 sc in each st, join to first sc made. End Color B. (12 sts)

ROUND 3: Join Color C, ch 1 and sc in same place, [ch 3, skip 1 st, sc in next st] 5 times, ch 3, join to first sc made. (6 sts, 6 ch sp)

ROUND 4: Sl st into ch-3 sp, ch 1, [(sc, hdc, dc, tr, dc, hdc, sc) in ch sp, sl st into next sc] 6 times, join to first sc made. End Color C. (6 petals)

ROUND 5: Join Color D, sl st into next 2 sts, sc in next st, * hdc in next st, (2 dc, ch 2, 2 dc) in next st, hdc in next st, sc in next st **, sl st in next 3 sts, sc in next st; rep from * 4 more times, then from * to ** once, sl st in next st. End Color D. (6 petals)

ROUND 6: Join Color A in middle sl st, ch 5 (counts as 1 dc, ch 2), dc in same place, [ch 3, (dc, ch 2, dc) in next middle sl st] 5 times, ch 3, join to 3rd ch of beginning ch. (12 sts, 12 ch sp)

ROUND 7: Ch 3 (counts as 1 dc), * (2 dc, ch 2, 2 dc) in ch-2 sp, dc in next st, 4 dc in ch-3 sp **, dc in next st; rep from * 4 more times, then from * to ** once, join to top of beginning ch. End Color A. (60 sts, 6 ch sp)

ROUND 8: Join Color B in next st, ch 2 (counts as 1 hdc), hdc in next st, * (hdc, dc, hdc) in ch-2 sp, hdc in next 2 sts, ch 2, skip 2 sts, 2 hdc into ch-2 sp of petal on Round 5 skipping 2 sts of current round, ch 2 **, hdc in next 2 sts; rep from * 4 more times, then from * to ** once, join to top of beginning ch. End Color B. (54 sts, 12 ch sp)

ROUND 9: Join Color E, ch 1 and sc in same place, sc in next 2 sts, * (sc, ch 1, sc) in next dc, sc in next 3 sts, sc into 2 skipped sts of Round 7 and ch-2 sp, sc in next 2 sts, sc in 2 skipped sts of Round 7 and ch-2 sp **, sc in next 3 sts; rep from * 4 more times, then from * to ** once, join to first sc made. End Color E. (84 sts, 6 ch sp)

ROUND 10: Join Color C, ch 1 and sc in same place, [sc in each st to corner ch-1 sp, (sc, ch 1, sc) in ch-1 sp] 6 times, sc in next 10 sts, join to first sc made. End Color C. (96 sts, 6 ch sp)

Pax Romana

- **SKILL LEVEL:** Advanced
- **SIZE OF HEXAGON:** 7 in. (18 cm)

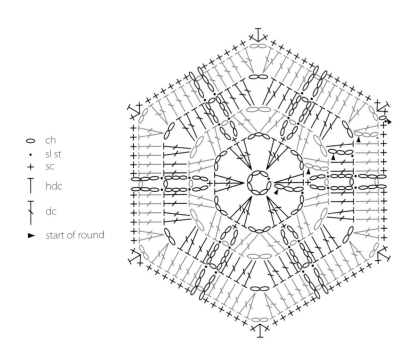

o	ch
•	sl st
+	sc
T	hdc
‡	dc
►	start of round

▨	A: 3.8 yd/3.5 m
▪	B: 3.8 yd/3.5 m
▫	C: 7.1 yd/6.5 m
▨	D: 9.8 yd/9 m
▪	E: 7.1 yd/6.5 m

Method

FOUNDATION RING: With Color A, ch 7 and join to form a ring.

ROUND 1: Ch 3 (counts as 1 dc), 2 dc into ring, [ch 3, 3 dc into ring] 5 times, ch 3, join to top of beginning ch. End Color A. (18 sts, 6 ch sp)

ROUND 2: Join Color B in next ch-3 sp, ch 3 (counts as 1 dc), (dc, ch 2, 2 dc) in same place, [ch 1, (2 dc, ch 2, 2 dc) in next ch-3 sp] 5 times, ch 1, join to top of beginning ch. End Color B. (24 sts, 12 ch sp)

ROUND 3: Join Color C in next ch-3 sp, ch 3 (counts as 1 dc), (dc, ch 2, 2 dc) in same place, * dc in each st to ch-1 sp, ch 1, skip ch sp, dc in each st to corner ch-2 sp **, (2 dc, ch 2, 2 dc) in ch-2 sp; rep from * 4 more times, then from * to ** once, join to top of beginning ch. End Color C. (48 sts, 12 ch sp)

ROUND 4: Join Color D in next ch-2 sp and repeat Round 3. End Color D. (72 sts, 12 ch sp)

ROUND 5: Join Color E in next ch-2 sp, ch 1, [(sc, hdc, sc) in ch-2 sp, sc in next 6 sts, ch 3, sl st around ch 1 of Round 3, ch 3, sl st around ch 1 of Round 2, ch 2, sc in middle of 3 dc group on Round 1, ch 2, sl st around ch 1 of Round 2, ch 3, sl st around ch 2 of Round 3, ch 3, sc in next 6 sts] 6 times, join to first sc made. End Color E. (96 sts)

Triangles

- **SKILL LEVEL:** Advanced
- **SIZE OF HEXAGON:** 5 in. (13 cm)

▢	A: 13.1 yd/12 m
◼	B: 5.5 yd/5 m
◼	C: 5.5 yd/5 m
◼	D: 5.5 yd/5 m

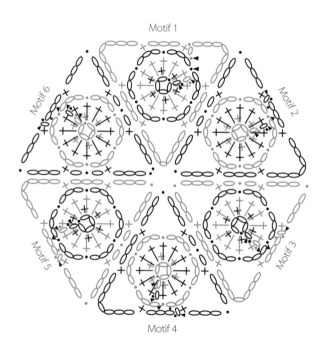

SPECIAL STITCH:
Spike sc: Worked over sts of previous round.

Method

MOTIF 1

FOUNDATION RING: With Color A, ch 4 and join to form a ring.

ROUND 1: Ch 1, 6 sc into ring, join to first sc made. (6 sts)

ROUND 2: Ch 1, 12 spike sc into ring, join to first sc made. End Color A. (12 sts)

ROUND 3: Join Color B, [ch 3, skip 1 st, sl st in next st] 6 times. (6 ch sp)

ROUND 4: Sl st into ch-3 sp, ch 1 and sc in same place, [ch 3, sc in next ch sp, ch 7, sc in next ch sp] twice, ch 3, sc in next ch sp, ch 7, join with sl st to first sc made. End Color B. (6 sts, 6 ch sp)

MOTIF 2

Work Rounds 1–3 as for Motif 1 using Color A for Rounds 1 and 2 and Color C for Round 3.

ROUND 4: Sl st into ch-3 sp, ch 1 and sc in same place, ch 3, sl st into 4th ch of corresponding ch 7 of previous motif, ch 3, sc in next ch-3 sp, ch 1, sl st into 2nd ch of corresponding ch 3, ch 1, sc in next ch-3 sp, ch 3, sl st into 4th ch of corresponding ch 7, ch 3, sc in next ch-3 sp, ch 3, sc in next ch-3 sp, ch 7, sc in next ch-3 sp, ch 3, join to first sc made. End Color C. (6 sts, 6 ch sp)

MOTIF 3

Repeat Motif 2 using Color A for Rounds 1 and 2 and Color D for Rounds 3 and 4.

MOTIF 4

Repeat Motif 2 using Color A for Rounds 1 and 2 and using Color B for Rounds 3 and 4.

MOTIF 5

Repeat Motif 2 using Color A for Rounds 1 and 2 and using Color C for Rounds 3 and 4.

MOTIF 6

Repeat Motif 2 using Color A for Rounds 1 and 2 and using Color D for Round 3.

ROUND 4: Sl st into ch-3 sp, ch 1 and sc in same place, ch 3, sl st into 4th of corresponding ch 7 of previous motif, * ch 3, sc in next ch-3 sp, ch 1, sl st into 2nd ch of corresponding ch 3, ch 1, sc in next ch-3 sp, ch 3 **, sl st into 4th ch of corresponding ch 7 of previous and next motifs; rep from * to ** once, sl st into 4th ch of corresponding ch 7 of next motif, ch 3, sc in next ch-3 sp, ch 3, join to first sc made. End Color D. (6 sts, 6 ch sp)

Motif 1

Motif 6

Motif 2

Motif 5

Motif 3

Motif 4

o	ch
•	sl st
+	sc
†	spike sc
►	start of round

Wild Rose

- **SKILL LEVEL:** Advanced
- **SIZE OF HEXAGON:** 7 in. (18 cm)

▨	A: 27.3 yd/25 m
▨	B: 5.5 yd/5 m
▨	C: 11 yd/10 m

Method

FOUNDATION RING: With Color A, ch 4 and join to form a ring.

ROUND 1: Ch 1, 12 sc into ring, join to first sc made. (12 sts)

ROUND 2: Ch 4 (counts as 1 dc, ch 1), [dc in next st, ch 1] 11 times, join to 3rd ch of beginning ch. (12 sts, 12 ch sp)

ROUND 3: Ch 4 (counts as 1 dc, ch 1), dc in same place, [ch 1, (dc, ch 1, dc) in next st] 11 times, ch 1, join to 3rd ch of beginning ch. (24 sts, 24 ch sp)

ROUND 4: Ch 5 (counts as 1 dc, ch 2), [dc in next st, ch 2] 23 times, join to 3rd ch of beginning ch. (24 sts, 24 ch sp)

ROUND 5: Sl st into ch-2 sp, ch 3 (counts as 1 dc), (dc, ch 2, 2 dc) in same place, * 2 hdc in next ch sp, 2 sc in next ch sp, 2 hdc in next ch sp **, (2 dc, ch 2, 2 dc) in next ch sp; rep from * 4 more times, then from * to ** once, join to top of beginning ch. (60 sts, 6 ch sp)

ROUND 6: Ch 5 (counts as 1 dc, ch 2), dc in same place, [dc in next 10 sts, (dc, ch 2, dc) in next ch-2 sp] 5 times, dc in next 10 sts, join to 3rd ch of beginning ch. End Color A. (72 sts, 6 ch sp)

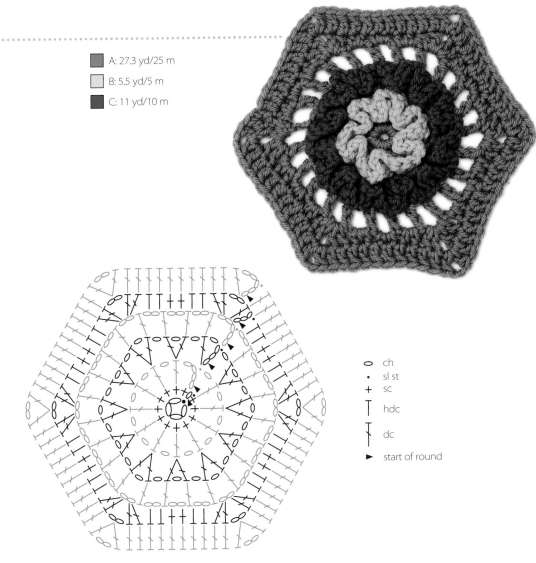

⬭	ch
•	sl st
+	sc
T	hdc
⊤	dc
►	start of round

Surface crochet repeat

SURFACE CROCHET

ROUND 1: With Color B, join yarn around any dc of Round 2, ch 3 (counts as 1 dc), 2 dc around same st working from bottom to top, *ch 2, 3 dc around next st starting at top of st and working down, ch 2 **, 3 dc around next st starting at bottom of st and working upward; rep from * 4 more times, then from * to ** once, join to top of beginning ch. End Color B.

ROUND 2: Join Color C on Round 4 and follow instructions for Round 1 but repeat from * 10 times and from * to ** once, join to top of beginning ch. End Color C.

PROJECT
Flower Bag

- **SKILL LEVEL:** Advanced
- **SIZE OF HEXAGON:** 5 in. (13 cm)
- **FINISHED SIZE:** 22 in. (56 cm) at widest point
- **HOOK SIZE:** J (5.5 mm)
- **YARN WEIGHT:** DK/light worsted
- **ADDITIONAL MATERIALS:** Two 7 in. (18 cm) diameter bamboo handles; 18 x 22 in. (45 x 56 cm) lining fabric (optional)

A: 50 yd/45.5 m
B: 85.5 yd/78 m
C: 185 yd/169 m
D: 252 yd/230 m

Method

Make 13 hexagons as follows:

FOUNDATION RING: With Color A, make a magic ring.

ROUND 1: Ch 1, 6 sc into ring, join to first sc made. (6 sts)

ROUND 2: Ch 1, (sc tfl, ch 5, sc tfl, ch 5) in same place, [(sc tfl, ch 5, sc tfl, ch 5) in next st] 5 times, join to first sc made. End Color A. (12 sts, 12 ch sp)

ROUND 3: Join Color B tbl of Round 1, ch 1, 2 sc tbl in same place, [2 sc tbl in next st] 5 times, join to first sc made. (12 sts)

ROUND 4: Ch 1, (sc tfl, ch 5, sc tfl, ch 5) in same place, [(sc tfl, ch 5, sc tfl, ch 5) in next st] 11 times, join to first sc made. End Color B. (24 sts, 24 ch sp)

ROUND 5: Join Color C tbl of Round 3, ch 1, sc tbl in same place, sc tbl in next 11 sts of Round 3, join to first sc made. (12 sts)

ROUND 6 (MAKE LEAF)

ROW 1: Ch 1, 3 sc in same place, turn.

ROW 2: Ch 1, 2 sc in first st, sc in next st, 2 sc in last st, turn.

ROW 3: Ch 1, 2 sc in first st, sc in next 3 sts, 2 sc in last st, turn.

ROW 4: Ch 1, sc2tog, sc in next 3 sts, sc2tog, turn.

ROW 5: Ch 1, sc2tog, sc in next st, sc2tog, turn.

ROW 6: Ch 1, sc2tog, sc in next st, turn.

ROW 7: Ch 1, sc2tog. End Color C.

[Skip 1 st of Round 5 and join yarn in next st, make leaf as before] 5 times. (6 leaves made)

ROUND 7: Join Color D in any skipped st on Round 5, ch 3 (counts as 1 dc), 2 dc in same place, [ch 2, 3 dc in next skipped st on Round 5] 5 times, ch 2, join to top of beginning ch. (18 sts, 6 ch sp)

ROUND 8: Ch 3 (counts as 1 dc), dc in next 2 sts, [(dc, ch 1, dc) in ch-2 sp, dc in next 3 sts] 5 times, (dc, ch 1, dc) in next ch-2 sp, join to top of beginning ch. (30 sts, 6 ch sp)

ROUND 9: Ch 3 (counts as 1 dc), dc in next 3 sts, [(dc, ch 2, dc) in ch-1 sp, dc in next 5 sts] 5 times, (dc, ch 2, dc) in ch-1 sp, dc in next st, join to top of beginning ch. (42 sts, 6 ch sp)

ROUND 10: Ch 1 and sc in same place, [sc in each st to corner ch-2 sp, (sc into ch-2 sp, hdc into top of Leaf, sc into ch-2 sp] 6 times, sc in next 2 sts, join to first sc made. End Color D. (60 sts)

Leaf

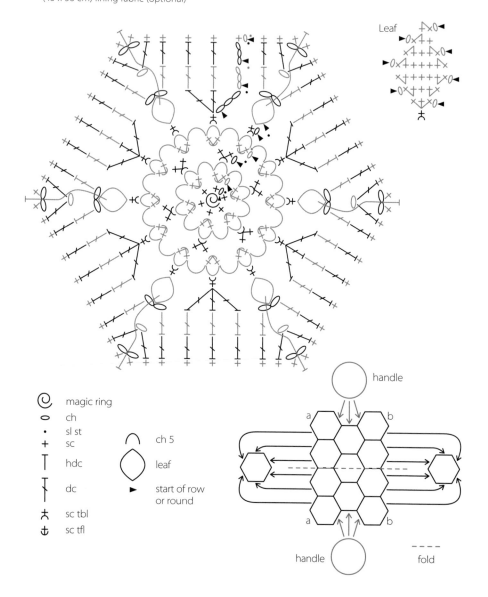

ⓒ magic ring
o ch
• sl st
+ sc
T hdc
Ŧ dc
⅄ sc tbl
⚓ sc tfl

⌒ ch 5
◇ leaf
► start of row or round

handle

a   b

a   b

handle   - - - - fold

JOINING THE HEXAGONS

Following the layout diagram and using Color D, join the hexagons using slip stitch through the back loops. Start with the central panel of 11 hexagons, then join the remaining 2 hexagons where arrows indicate. Fold the bag and join sides marked "a" together, then join sides marked "b" together.

FINISHING

With Color D, work a round of sc around the top opening of the bag, working 3 sc in outward-facing hexagon corners and sc2tog in inward-facing corners. End Color D, then rejoin it in the middle st of the right-hand outward-facing corner. Ch 2, then holding the handle at the back of all sts, work 1 sc into next 32 sts working around the handle. Repeat for other handle.

If you wish, use the crochet bag to draw a template for lining fabric. Fold the fabric in half and cut out around the template. Stitch the side edges of the fabric together, then hem around the top. Hand stitch the top of the lining to the crochet fabric with thread to match Color D.

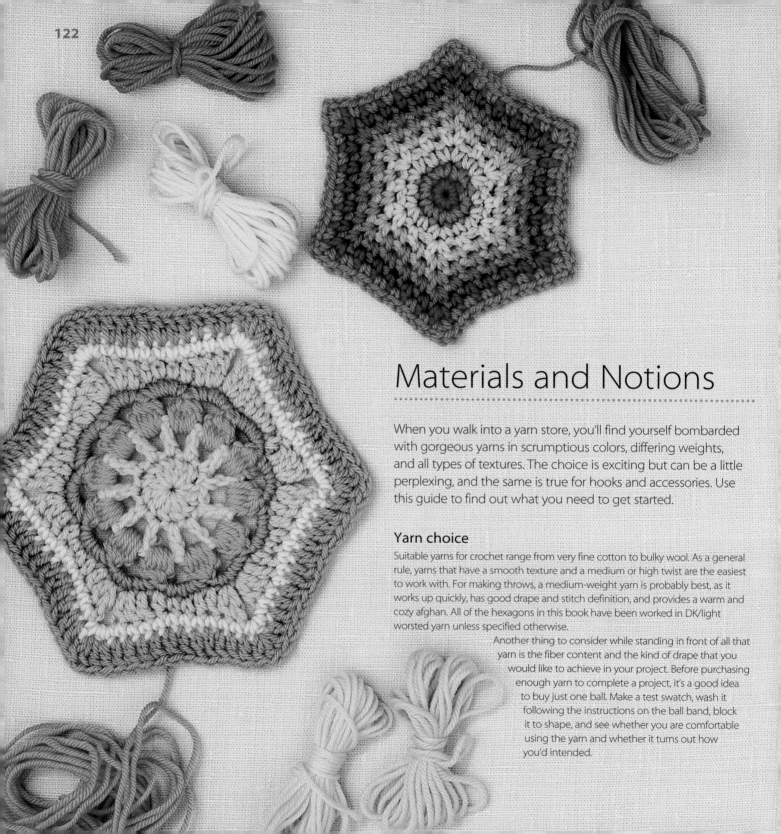

Materials and Notions

When you walk into a yarn store, you'll find yourself bombarded with gorgeous yarns in scrumptious colors, differing weights, and all types of textures. The choice is exciting but can be a little perplexing, and the same is true for hooks and accessories. Use this guide to find out what you need to get started.

Yarn choice

Suitable yarns for crochet range from very fine cotton to bulky wool. As a general rule, yarns that have a smooth texture and a medium or high twist are the easiest to work with. For making throws, a medium-weight yarn is probably best, as it works up quickly, has good drape and stitch definition, and provides a warm and cozy afghan. All of the hexagons in this book have been worked in DK/light worsted yarn unless specified otherwise.

Another thing to consider while standing in front of all that yarn is the fiber content and the kind of drape that you would like to achieve in your project. Before purchasing enough yarn to complete a project, it's a good idea to buy just one ball. Make a test swatch, wash it following the instructions on the ball band, block it to shape, and see whether you are comfortable using the yarn and whether it turns out how you'd intended.

Yarn fibers

Yarns come in a range of different fibers and fiber combinations.

WOOL

Wool is an excellent choice for throws. It is a resilient fiber that feels good to crochet with and has great stitch definition. If you are making a project that you would like to hand down to future generations and it is within your budget, wool is the fiber to use. Do find out whether or not the wool can be machine washed.

ACRYLIC

Acrylic yarn is a perfect choice for beginners and popular with crochet enthusiasts. It's great for practicing stitches and techniques and testing color combinations. Acrylic yarns come in a huge array of colors and it is an affordable choice for your first project. Although acrylic can pill and lose its shape eventually, it does have the benefit of being machine-washable, making it a good choice for items that may require frequent washing.

COMBINATION YARNS

A yarn comprised of both wool and synthetic fiber is a dependable choice. Picking something that has a small percentage of synthetic fiber (for example, nylon or acrylic) makes a nice yarn to work with and launder, while still retaining the advantages of wool.

COTTON AND COTTON MIXES

Cotton can present more of a challenge for beginners. It can be a little stiff to work with, but the stitches are crisp and neat. A cotton mix is usually softer to work with, yet still retains crisp, neat stitch definition. Throws crocheted with cotton or a cotton mix are durable and cool, so are perfect for summer.

NOVELTY YARNS

Although novelty yarns are tactile and enticing, they are not easy to work with. You can use a splash of novelty yarn to add some interest, but on the whole they are tricky to use and also hide the stitches.

Crochet hooks

Hooks come in different sizes and materials. The material a hook is made from can affect your gauge. To start out, it's best to use aluminum hooks, as they have a pointed head and well-defined throat and work well with most yarns. Bamboo hooks are also pleasing to work with, but can be slippery with some yarns. Plastic hooks can be squeaky with synthetic yarns. You can also purchase hooks with soft-grip or wooden handles, which are great to work with, particularly if crochet becomes an obsession.

WHAT SIZE?

You may find that using the hook size recommended for a particular yarn or pattern isn't satisfactory, and your work may be too tight or too loose. Try different hook sizes until you are happy with the completed swatch. Ultimately, you want to use a hook and yarn weight that you are comfortable with—yarn/hook recommendations are not set in stone. Be aware that not all yarn labels give a recommended hook size. Use the recommended knitting needle size as a guide, or a hook one or two sizes bigger.

Notions

Although all you need to get started is a hook and some yarn, it's handy to have the following items in your work bag.

NEEDLES

Yarn or tapestry needles are used for sewing seams and weaving in yarn tails. Choose needles with blunt ends to avoid splitting stitches. Yarn needles have different-sized eyes, so choose one that will accommodate the weight of yarn you will be using.

PINS

Use rustproof, glass-headed pins for wet and steam blocking.

STITCH MARKERS

Split-ring markers are handy for keeping track of the first stitch of a row, particularly when starting out. Also use them to hold the working loop when you put your work down for the night.

SCISSORS

Use a pair of small, sharp embroidery scissors.

RULER AND MEASURING TAPE

A rigid ruler is best for measuring gauge. A sturdy measuring tape is good for taking larger measurements.

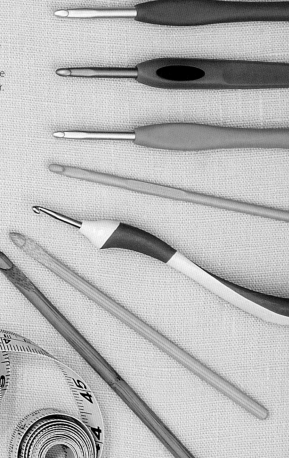

Basic Stitches and Techniques

All crochet stitches are based on a loop pulled through another loop by a hook. There are only a few stitches to master, each of a different length. Crochet can be worked in rows, beginning with a foundation chain, or in rounds, working outward from a foundation ring of chain stitches or a magic ring. Practice making chains and working the basic stitches before moving on to more challenging techniques.

Holding the hook and yarn

The most common way of holding the hook is shown below, but if this doesn't feel comfortable to you, try grasping the flat section of the hook between your thumb and forefinger as if you were holding a knife.

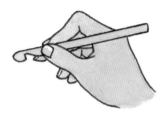

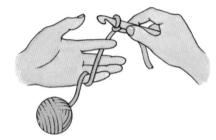

1 Holding the hook like a pen is the most widely used method. Center the tips of your right thumb and forefinger over the flat section of the hook.

2 To control the supply and keep an even tension on the yarn, loop the short end of the yarn over your left forefinger, and take the yarn coming from the ball loosely around the little finger on the same hand. Use the middle finger on the same hand to help hold the work. If you are left-handed, hold the hook in your left hand and the yarn in your right.

Making a slip knot

1 Loop the yarn as shown, insert the hook into the loop, catch the yarn with the hook, and pull it through to make a loop over the hook.

2 Gently pull the yarn to tighten the loop around the hook and complete the slip knot.

Foundation chain

The foundation chain is the equivalent of casting on in knitting, and it is important to make sure that you have made the required number of chains for the pattern you are going to work. Count each V-shaped loop on the front of the chain as one chain stitch, except for the loop on the hook, which is not counted. If your chain stitches are tight, try using a larger hook for the foundation chain.

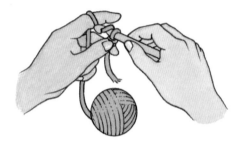

1 Holding the hook with the slip knot in your right hand and the yarn in your left hand, wrap the yarn over the hook. Draw the yarn through to make a new loop and complete the first chain stitch.

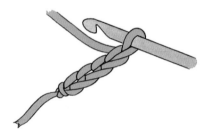

2 Repeat this process, drawing a new loop of yarn through the loop already on the hook until the foundation chain is the required length. After every few stitches, move up the thumb and finger that are grasping the chain to keep the chain stitches even.

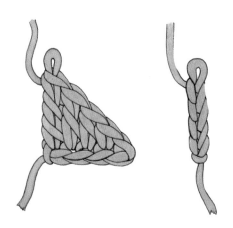

Turning and starting chains

When working crochet in rows or rounds, you will need to work a specific number of extra chains at the beginning of each row or round. When the work is turned at the end of a straight row, the extra chains are called a turning chain, and when they are worked at the beginning of a round, they are called a starting chain.

The extra chains bring the hook up to the correct height for the stitch you will be working next. The turning or starting chain is counted as the first stitch of the row or round, except when working single crochet where the single turning chain is ignored. A chain may be longer than the number required for the stitch, and in that case counts as one stitch plus a number of chains. At the end of the row or round, the final stitch is usually worked into the turning chain at the beginning of the previous row or round. The final stitch may be worked into the top chain of the turning or starting chain or into another specified stitch of the chain.

Single crochet (sc): *1 turning chain*
Half double crochet (hdc): *2 turning chains*
Double crochet (dc): *3 turning chains*
Treble crochet (tr): *4 turning chains*
Double treble crochet (dtr): *5 turning chains*
Triple treble crochet (trtr): *6 turning chains*

Slip stitch (sl st)

Slip stitch is the shortest of all the crochet stitches and its main uses are joining stitches and carrying the hook and yarn from one place to another.

Insert the hook from front to back into the required stitch. Wrap the yarn over the hook and draw it through both the work and the loop on the hook. One loop remains on the hook and one slip stitch has been worked.

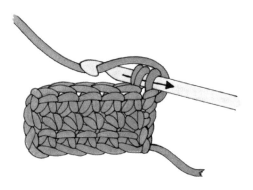

Single crochet (sc)

1 Begin with a foundation chain and insert the hook from front to back into the second chain from the hook. Wrap the yarn over the hook and draw it through the first loop, leaving two loops on the hook.

2 To complete the stitch, wrap the yarn over the hook and draw it through both loops on the hook, leaving one loop on the hook. Continue in this way, working one single crochet into each chain.

3 At the end of the row, turn and work one chain for the turning chain (remember that this chain does not count as a stitch). Insert the hook into the first single crochet at the beginning of the row. Work a single crochet into each stitch of the previous row, working the final stitch into the last stitch of the row (not into the turning chain).

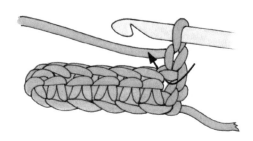

Half double crochet (hdc)

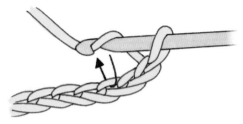

1 Begin with a foundation chain. Wrap the yarn over the hook and insert the hook into the third chain from the hook.

2 Draw the yarn through the chain, leaving three loops. Wrap the yarn over the hook and draw it through all three loops on the hook, leaving one loop on the hook.

3 Continue along the row, working one half double crochet into each chain. At the end of the row, turn and work two chains for the turning chain. Skip the first stitch and work a half double crochet into each remaining stitch along the row. Work the final stitch into the top of the turning chain.

Double crochet (dc)

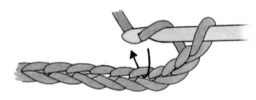

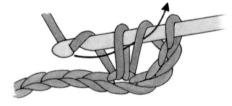

1 Begin with a foundation chain, then wrap the yarn over the hook and insert the hook into the fourth chain from the hook.

2 Draw the yarn through the chain, leaving three loops on the hook. Wrap the yarn again and draw it through the first two loops on the hook, leaving two loops on the hook.

3 Wrap the yarn over the hook and draw it through the two loops on the hook, leaving one loop on the hook. Repeat along the row. At the end of the row, turn and work three turning chains. Skip the first stitch and work a double crochet into each remaining stitch along the row. Work the final stitch into the top of the turning chain.

Treble crochet (tr)

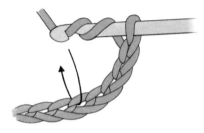

1 Begin with a foundation chain. Wrap the yarn over the hook twice and insert the hook into the fifth chain from the hook.

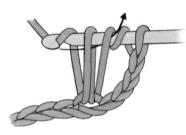

2 Draw the yarn through the chain, leaving four loops on the hook. Wrap the yarn again and draw it through the first two loops on the hook, leaving three loops on the hook.

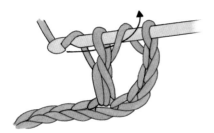

3 Wrap the yarn again and draw it through the first two loops on the hook, leaving two loops on the hook.

4 Wrap the yarn again and draw it through the two remaining loops, leaving one loop on the hook. Continue along the row, working one treble crochet stitch into each chain. At the end of the row, turn and work four chains for the turning chain. Skip the first stitch and work a treble crochet into each stitch along the row. At the end of the row, work the last stitch into the top of the turning chain.

Double treble crochet (dtr)

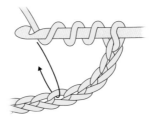

1 Begin with a foundation chain. Wrap the yarn over the hook three times and insert the hook into the sixth chain from the hook.

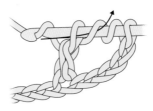

3 Wrap the yarn again and draw it through the first two loops on the hook, leaving three loops on the hook.

5 Wrap the yarn again and draw it through the two remaining loops, leaving one loop on the hook to complete the stitch. Work five turning chains for a double treble at the beginning of a row; work the final stitch of the row into the top of the turning chain.

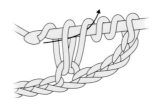

2 Draw the yarn through the chain, leaving five loops on the hook. Wrap the yarn again and draw it through the first two loops on the hook, leaving four loops on the hook.

4 Wrap the yarn again and draw it through the first two loops on the hook, leaving two loops on the hook.

Triple treble crochet (trtr)

Work in the same way as double treble crochet, but start by wrapping the yarn over the hook four times instead of three. Work off two loops at a time in the usual way. Work six turning chains for a triple treble at the beginning of a row; work the final stitch of the row into the top of the turning chain.

Working in rounds—starting off

Crochet worked in rounds is worked outward from a central ring of chains, called a foundation ring, or from a magic ring.

USING A FOUNDATION RING

1 Work a short length of foundation chain as specified in the pattern. Join the chains into a ring by working a slip stitch into the first chain of the foundation chain.

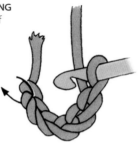

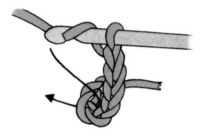

2 Work the number of starting chains specified in the pattern—three chains are shown here (counting as one double crochet stitch). Inserting the hook into the space at the center of the ring each time, work the number of stitches specified in the pattern.

3 Count the stitches at the end of the round to check that you have worked the correct number. Join the first and last stitches of the round together by working a slip stitch into the top (or other specified stitch) of the starting chain.

USING A MAGIC RING

A magic ring can be used in place of a foundation ring for crocheting in the round. The benefit of this method is that, after pulling the yarn tail to draw the stitches together, there is no hole at the center of your work.

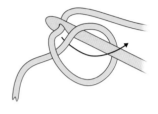

1 Wrap the yarn into a ring, leaving the yarn tail on the left and the working yarn on the right. Insert the hook and catch the yarn to pull through.

2 Draw a loop of the working yarn through the magic ring.

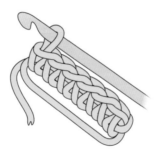

4 Continue in the same manner as for working into a foundation ring, but this time work the stitches into the magic ring.

3 Now work the number of starting chains required in the pattern.

5 When the first round is complete, pull tightly on the yarn tail to close the magic ring. Join the ends of the round with a slip stitch.

Finishing off the final round

For a really neat edge on the final round, use this method of sewing the first and last stitches together in preference to using a slip stitch.

1 Cut the yarn, leaving a tail of about 4 in. (10 cm), and draw it through the last stitch. With right side facing, thread the tail in a yarn needle and take it under both loops of the stitch next to the starting chain.

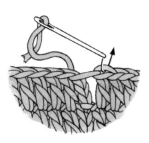

2 Insert the needle into the center of the last stitch of the round. On the wrong side, pull the needle through to complete the stitch, adjust the length of the stitch to close the round, then weave in the tail on the wrong side and trim.

Joining a new color

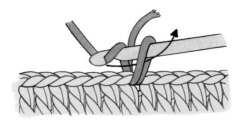

WHEN WORKING IN THE ROUND
When the pattern states "Join Color B," this is done in the same place that the old yarn ended, usually at the start of a round. To join a new color, insert the hook in the work as instructed, draw up a loop of the new color leaving a tail about 4 in. (10 cm) long, and chain 1. Continue with the new yarn.

AT THE START OR IN THE MIDDLE OF A ROW
When working the last stitch of the old color, leave the final stage of the stitch incomplete, wrap the new color around the hook, and finish the stitch with the new color.

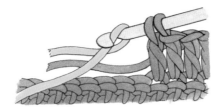

1 Draw the new color through the last two loops of the stitch.

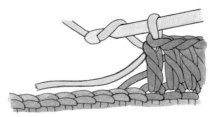

2 Continue working in the new color.

Decreases

One or two stitches can be decreased by working two or three incomplete stitches together, and the method is the same for all the basic crochet stitches.

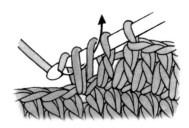

1 To work two stitches together, leave the first stitch incomplete so there are two loops on the hook, then work another incomplete stitch so you have three loops on the hook.

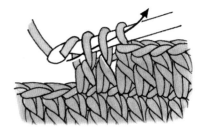

2 Wrap the yarn and draw it through all three loops to finish the decrease. Two stitches can be decreased in the same way by working three stitches together. When working in double crochet, for example, this decrease is called dc2tog or dc3tog.

Stitch Variations

Basic stitches may be varied in many ways to achieve different effects—for example, by working several stitches in the same place to make clusters and bobbles, or by inserting the hook in a different place. You can also work crochet across the surface of the finished piece to create really dazzling designs.

Cluster (CL)

A cluster is made by working a multiple of any of the basic crochet stitches, leaving the last loop of each stitch on the hook until they are worked together at the end. Count the turning or starting chain as the first stitch.

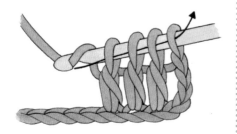

1 Work the first crochet stitch of the cluster, omitting the last stage to leave two loops on the hook. Work the remaining stitches in the same way, leaving the last loop of each stitch on the hook. So to make a 4 dc cluster with the turning chain forming the first stitch, as here, you will have four loops on the hook. Wrap the yarn over the hook once more.

2 Draw the yarn through all four loops to complete the cluster and secure the stitch.

Slanting cluster (SCL)

A slanting cluster is made by working a cluster of half double crochet stitches around the previous stitch.

1 Wrap the yarn over the hook, insert the hook from right to left around the post (stem) of the previous stitch, wrap the yarn over the hook, and draw up a loop. Repeat twice more until seven loops are on the hook.

2 Wrap the yarn over the hook and draw it through all seven loops on the hook.

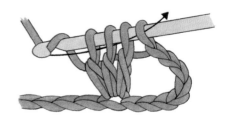

Bobble (BO)

A bobble is a group of between three and six double crochet or longer stitches worked into the same stitch and closed at the top. Bobbles are worked on wrong-side rows and they are usually surrounded by shorter stitches to throw them into high relief. At the beginning of a row or round, the pattern may count the turning or starting chain as the first stitch of the bobble. When working bobbles in a contrasting color, use a separate length of yarn to make each bobble, carrying the main yarn under the bobble stitches or across the back of the bobble.

To make a three-stitch bobble, work three double crochet stitches into the same stitch, omitting the final stage of each stitch so that the last loop of each one remains on the hook. You now have four loops on the hook. Wrap the yarn over the hook and draw it through the four loops to secure them and complete the bobble.

Popcorn (PC)

A popcorn is a group of double crochet or longer stitches (the number of stitches may vary) sharing the same base stitch, which is folded and closed at the top so that the popcorn is raised from the background stitches. At the beginning of a row or round, the pattern may count the turning or starting chain as the first stitch of the popcorn.

1 To make a popcorn with four stitches, work a group of four double crochet stitches into the same place.

2 Take the hook out of the working loop and insert it under both loops of the first double crochet in the group. Pick up the working loop with the hook and draw it through to fold the group of stitches and close it at the top.

Puff stitch (PS)

A puff stitch is a cluster of half double crochet stitches worked in the same place (the number of stitches may vary). At the beginning of a row or round, the pattern may count the turning or starting chain as the first stitch of the puff.

1 Wrap the yarn over the hook, insert the hook where required, and draw a loop through (three loops on the hook). Repeat this step twice more, inserting the hook into the same stitch (seven loops on the hook).

2 Wrap the yarn over the hook and draw it through all seven loops on the hook. Work an extra chain stitch at the top of the puff to complete the stitch.

Bullion stitch

A bullion stitch is formed by wrapping the yarn several times (normally seven to ten) around the hook and pulling a loop through.

Wrap the yarn (not too tightly) as many times as directed around the hook. Insert the hook where required and draw through a loop. Wrap the yarn over the hook again and draw it through all the loops on the hook. You can ease each loop in turn off the hook, rather than try to pull through all of them at once.

Standing stitches

Standing stitches are used instead of working a starting chain. Rather than beginning at the bottom of the stitch, you begin at the top. Any stitch can be worked in this way.

Begin with a slip knot on the hook, then work the required stitch directly into the place indicated in the pattern. When you have completed the stitch, the slip knot will be at the top. At the end of the round, join the first and last stitches of the round together by working a slip stitch into the slip knot at the top of the standing stitch.

Working into one loop

If the hook is inserted under just one loop at the top of a stitch, the empty loop creates a ridge on either the front or the back of the fabric. Throughout this book, "front loop" means the loop nearest to you, at the top of the stitch, and "back loop" means the farther loop, whether you are working a right-side or a wrong-side row.

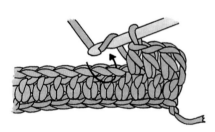

THROUGH FRONT LOOP (TFL)
If the hook is inserted under the front loop only, the empty back loop will show as a ridge on the other side of the work.

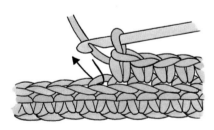

THROUGH BACK LOOP (TBL)
If the hook is inserted under the back loop only, the empty front loop creates a ridge on the side of the work facing you.

Working through the horizontal bar (thb)

This technique is much the same as working into the front or back loop only. Working into the bar at the back of each stitch raises the front and back loops to add some textural interest.

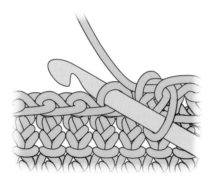

1 Fold the stitches forward and insert the hook from top to bottom through the horizontal bar or "bump" at the back of the specified stitch.

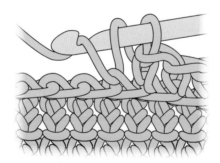

2 Continue working the stitch as normal.

Working around posts

This technique creates raised stitches by inserting the hook around the post (stem) of the stitch, from the front or the back.

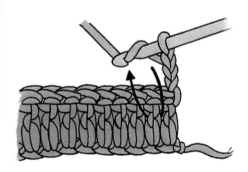

AROUND FRONT POST (FP)
Wrap the yarn over the hook from back to front, insert the hook from the front to the back at right of the next stitch, then bring it to the front at the left of the same stitch. Complete the stitch in the usual way.

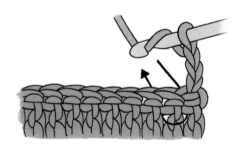

AROUND BACK POST (BP)
Wrap the yarn over the hook, insert the hook from the back to the front at right of the next stitch, then take it back again at the left of the same stitch. Complete the stitch in the usual way.

Inserting the hook in other places

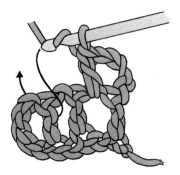

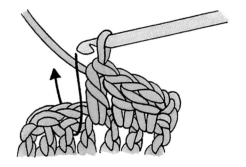

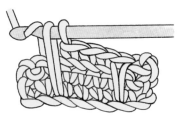

WORKING INTO A CHAIN SPACE (CH SP)
The hook is inserted into the space below one or more chains. Here, a treble crochet stitch is being worked into a chain-1 space.

INSERTING BETWEEN STITCHES
Here, the hook is inserted between the stitches of the previous row, instead of at the top of a stitch.

WORKING INTO LOWER ROWS TO MAKE SPIKE STITCHES
Spike stitches are made by inserting the hook one or more rows below the previous row, either directly below the next stitch or to the left or right. To work a single crochet spike stitch, for example, insert the hook as directed by the pattern, wrap the yarn over the hook and draw it through, lengthen the loop to the height of the working row, then complete the stitch.

Surface crochet

Surface crochet is worked onto the crochet hexagon when it is complete; the stitches used are usually chain stitch or single crochet and can be used to "draw" lines, swirls, and letters. You can also work other stitches on the surface of the fabric, such as double crochet. Work around the posts of stitches or through the gaps between stitches.

1 Holding the working yarn at the back of the hexagon at all times, insert the hook from front to back through the fabric in a space between two stitches and pull through a loop.

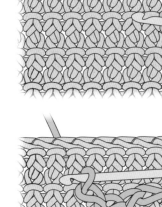

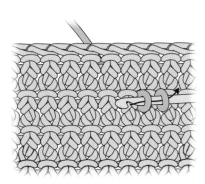

2 Insert the hook from front to back in the space between the next two stitches and pull up another loop.

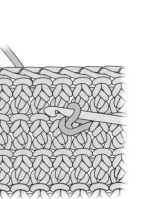

3 Pull the second loop through the first loop on the hook to make a chain stitch.

4 Continue in this way, working chain stitches to form a pattern. When complete, secure the yarn ends.

Reading Patterns and Charts

With all those symbols, abbreviations, and charts, crochet can seem daunting and complex to begin with. A little explanation, though, and all becomes clear.

Crochet can use a number of different stitches, so to make patterns quicker and easier to follow, abbreviations are used. Abbreviations and symbols may vary from one pattern publisher to another, so always check that you understand the system in use before commencing work. Some patterns use special abbreviations, which are explained with the pattern.

SYMBOLS

Symbol	Stitch or term
*	Start of repeat
**	End of last repeat
[ ]	Repeat the instructions within the brackets the stated number of times
( )	Can either be explanatory (counts as 1 dc) or can be read as a group of stitches worked into the same stitch or space (dc, ch 2, dc)
►	An arrowhead indicates the beginning of a row or round

ARRANGEMENTS OF SYMBOLS

Symbols joined at top
A group of symbols may be joined at the top, indicating that these stitches should be worked together at the top, as in cluster stitches, and for decreasing the number of stitches (e.g. sc2tog, dc3tog).

Symbols joined at base
Symbols joined at the base should all be worked into the same stitch below.

Symbols joined at top and base
Sometimes a group of stitches are joined at both top and bottom, making a puff, bobble, or popcorn.

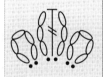

Symbols on a curve
Sometimes symbols are drawn at an angle, depending on the construction of the stitch pattern.

Distorted symbols
Some symbols may be lengthened, curved, or spiked, to indicate where the hook is inserted below.

ABBREVIATIONS

Symbol	Stitch or term	Abbreviation
	Magic ring	
	Chain	ch
	Slip stitch	sl st
	Single crochet	sc
	Half double crochet	hdc
	Double crochet	dc
	Treble crochet	tr
	Double treble crochet	dtr
	Triple treble crochet	trtr
	Cluster	CL
e.g. bobble of 5 doubles	Bobble	BO
e.g. puff of 5 half doubles	Puff stitch	PS
e.g. popcorn of 5 doubles	Popcorn	PC
e.g. single through back loop	Through back loop	tbl
e.g. half double through front loop	Through front loop	tfl
e.g. single through horizontal bar	Through horizontal bar	thb
	Back post	BP
	Front post	FP
	Chain space	ch sp
	Together	tog
	Yarn over	yo
	Beginning	beg
	Repeat	rep

Reading charts

Each design in this book is accompanied by a chart, which should be read together with the written instructions. Once you are used to the symbols, they are quick and easy to follow. All charts are read from the right side.

CHARTS IN ROWS
• Right-side rows start at the right, and are read from right to left.
• Wrong-side rows start at the left, and are read from left to right.
• The beginning of each row is indicated by an arrow.

CHARTS IN ROUNDS
These charts begin at the center, and each round is read counterclockwise, in the same direction as working. The beginning of each round is indicated by an arrow. Some charts have been stretched to show all the stitches.

SURFACE CROCHET
Surface crochet is provided as a separate chart where necessary and is worked after the fabric has been completed.

CALCULATING YARN AMOUNTS

Each of the patterns in this book provides the amount of yarn required. This yardage is approximate and based on using DK/light worsted yarn and a size H (5 mm) hook unless specified otherwise. The best way to calculate how much yarn you will need is to make a few hexagons in the yarn and color combination you intend to use, then unravel them. Measure the amount of yarn used for each color, take the average yardage, and multiply by the number of hexagons you intend to make. Add extra yarn for joining the hexagons and working edgings.

Gauge

It's important to crochet a test swatch before you start your project to establish gauge.

No two people will crochet to the exact same gauge, even when working with identical yarn and hooks. Gauge can be affected by the type of hook you use, the type of yarn you choose, how you hold the hook, and how the yarn feeds through your fingers. Beginners tend to have a tight gauge, so may benefit from using a larger hook than the pattern recommends.

Always make a test swatch before you start your project. Your test swatch will allow you to compare your gauge with the pattern gauge and will give you a good idea of how the finished project will feel and drape. It's also useful for testing out color combinations. All of the swatches in this book have been worked in DK/light worsted yarn using a size H (5 mm) crochet hook unless specified otherwise. To test your gauge, make a sample swatch in the yarn you intend to use following the pattern directions. The hexagon should measure a little less than the finished size to allow for blocking. Block the sample hexagon and then measure again. If your hexagon is larger, try making another hexagon using a smaller hook. If your hexagon is smaller, try making another hexagon using a bigger hook. Also do this if the fabric feels too loose and floppy or too dense and rigid. Keep trying until you find a hook size that will give you the required gauge, or until you are happy with the drape and feel of your work. Ultimately, it's more important that you use a hook and yarn you are comfortable with than that you rigidly follow the pattern instructions.

MULTIPLE USES: *Keep a gauge swatch to test blocking and cleaning methods.*

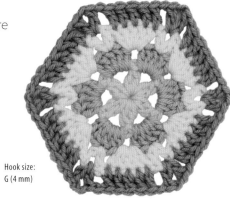

Hook size:
G (4 mm)

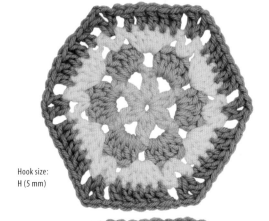

Hook size:
H (5 mm)

Hook size:
J (6 mm)

Swatches shown at 45 percent actual size

Blocking and Joining

To finish off your hexagons neatly, you'll need to block them before using one of the joining methods. You can choose to sew or crochet your hexagons together, and opt for either a visible join at the front of your work or keeping it out of sight at the back. A single-crochet join in a contrasting color to your hexagons can add texture and interest. A woven seam can be used if you don't want the join to be seen.

Blocking

Blocking is crucial to set the stitches and even out the hexagons ready for joining. Choose a method based on the care label of your yarn or, if none is provided, take into account the fiber content. When in doubt, use the wet method. Use an ironing board, pillow, or old quilt. Or, you may find it useful to make a blocking board by securing one or two layers of quilter's batting, covered with a sheet of cotton fabric, over a piece of flat board.

WET METHOD—ACRYLIC AND WOOL/ACRYLIC BLENDS

Using rustproof pins, pin your hexagons to the correct measurements on a flat surface and dampen using a spray bottle of cold water. Pat the fabric to help the moisture penetrate more easily. Ease stitches into position, keeping rows and stitches straight. Allow to dry before removing the pins.

STEAM METHOD—WOOLS AND COTTONS

With wrong sides facing up, pin the hexagons to the correct measurements using rustproof pins. For hexagons with raised stitches, pin them with right sides facing up to avoid squashing the stitches. Steam lightly, holding the iron 1 in. (2.5 cm) above your work. Allow the steam to penetrate the hexagons for several seconds. It is safer to avoid pressing, but if you choose to do so, cover with a clean towel or cloth first and press lightly to avoid flattening the stitches. Allow to dry before removing the pins.

Joining with seams

Hexagons can be joined together by sewing or by crochet. Place markers and pin seams together to help match up the hexagons and give a neat finish. Use the same yarn that you used for the hexagons, or a finer yarn, preferably with the same fiber content.

OVERCAST SEAM

Pieces of crochet can be joined by overcasting the seam. The overcasting stitches (also known as whip stitches) can be worked through just the back of the crochet loops or the whole loops. Place the hexagons side by side on a flat surface with right sides up and edges together. Thread a large, blunt-ended sewing needle with yarn.

1 Working from right to left, overcast the seam by inserting the needle into the back loop of corresponding stitches. For extra strength, you can work two stitches into the end loops.

2 Continue overcasting the seam, making sure you join only the back loops of the edges together, until you reach the end of the seam. Secure the yarn at the beginning and end of the stitching.

BACKSTITCH SEAM

A backstitch seam creates a strong but non-elastic seam and is suitable where firmness is required and for lightweight yarns. With right sides facing, pin together the hexagons, inserting the pins at right angles to the edge. Thread a large, blunt-ended sewing needle with yarn.

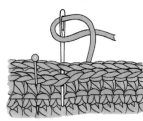

1 Secure the end of the seam and yarn by taking the needle twice around the outer edges of the fabric, from back to front. Take the yarn around the outside edge once more, but this time insert the needle through the work from back to front no more than ½ in. (1.3 cm) from where the yarn last emerged. Insert the needle from front to back where the first stitch began, then bring the needle through to the front again, the same distance along the edge as before.

2 Work in backstitch from right to left along the whole seam, staying close to the edge and going through both pieces of fabric. Secure the end with a couple of overlapping stitches.

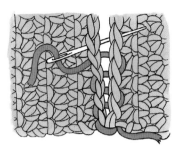

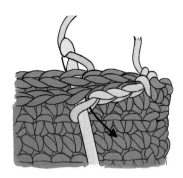

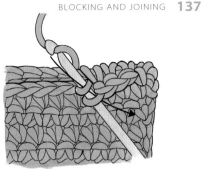

MATTRESS STITCH/WOVEN STITCH
Place the pieces to be joined side by side on a flat surface, wrong sides up and edges together. Thread a large, blunt-ended sewing needle with yarn. Starting at the bottom and working from right to left, place the needle under the loop of the first stitch on both pieces and draw the yarn through. Move up one stitch and repeat this process, going from left to right. Continue to zigzag loosely from edge to edge. Pull the yarn tight every inch or so, allowing the edges to join together. A woven seam gives a flatter finish than a backstitch seam and works better for baby garments and fine work.

SLIP STITCH CROCHET SEAM
A slip stitch crochet seam can be worked with right sides together, and will form a ridge at the back of the work. Or, work with wrong sides together for a ridge on the right side of the work. This can be effective worked in a different color from the hexagons.

Hold the pieces with right sides facing. You can work through both loops (as above), which creates a thick seam, or through one loop for a less bulky seam. Insert the hook under the back loop only of the nearest edge and the front loop only of the farther edge.

SINGLE CROCHET SEAM
Work as for the slip stitch seam, but in single crochet. Again, this is a method that can be used at the front or back of the work.

WEAVING IN ENDS

At the end of making your project, you will need to weave in any yarn tails from changing colors and sewing seams. For crochet worked in rows, sew in ends diagonally on the wrong side. For crochet worked in rounds, sew in ends under stitches for a couple of inches. If the pattern doesn't allow this, sew under a few stitches, then up through the back of a stitch, and under a few more stitches on the next row.

Joining as you go
If the last round of a hexagon has chain spaces along the edges, you can join-as-you-go on subsequent hexagons. Where two hexagons join, you will work a slip stitch into the adjacent hexagon rather than working a chain space. Work the first hexagon as the pattern indicates.

JOINING ALONG ONE SIDE
On the last round of the second hexagon, work to a corner chain space. Work the number of chains required for the corner minus one chain in the middle. At the middle, work a slip stitch into the corner chain space of the first hexagon. If there are only two chains at the corner, work the first chain and then work a slip stitch into the corner space of the first hexagon instead of working the second chain. Reverse these directions when you reach the next corner.

Continue working the stitches along the side of the second hexagon until you come to where the pattern calls for a chain space. Slip stitch into the corresponding chain space on the first hexagon. Contine working the stitches and slip stitches to the next corner. Slip stitch into the corresponding corner space of the first hexagon as before.

JOINING ALONG TWO OR MORE SIDES
Join as above until you reach the corner where three hexagons meet. For a corner with two chains, slip stitch into the first hexagon (instead of the first chain stitch) and then slip stitch into the corner of the second hexagon (instead of the second chain stitch). When there are more than two chains in a corner, work the number of chains required to reach the middle chain. Instead of working the middle chain, slip stitch into the first hexagon, slip stitch into the second hexagon, and then continue working the remaining corner chains.

You can add a round to any hexagon to make a join-as-you-go hexagon, such as on the Baby Blanket project (page 46).

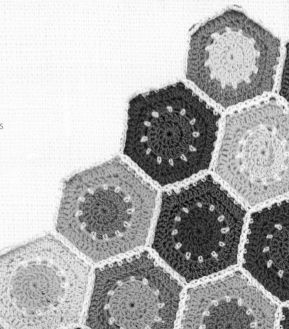

Half Hexagons

When making a project, you may want to include some half hexagons to fill in the edges, such as for a straight-edged throw. You can adapt most hexagons into half hexagons with a bit of "fudging" (see panel opposite). If that seems a bit technical and fiddly, though, here are some half hexagons you can use, all suitable for beginners.

7 in. (18 cm)

FOUNDATION ROW: With Color A, ch 2 (counts as 1 foundation ch, ch 1).

ROW 1: 4 sc into foundation ch. End Color A. (4 sts)

ROW 2: Join Color B in first sc of previous row, ch 3 (counts as 1 dc), dc in same place, [2 dc in next st] 3 times. End Color B. (8 sts)

ROW 3: Join Color C in first st of previous row, ch 3 (counts as 1 dc), dc in same place, dc in next st, (dc, ch 2, dc) in next st, dc in next 2 sts, (dc, ch 2, dc) in next st, dc in next st, 2 dc in last st. End Color C. (12 sts, 2 ch sp)

ROW 4: Join Color D in first st of previous row, ch 3 (counts as 1 dc), dc in same place, dc in next 3 sts, (dc, ch 2, dc) in ch-2 sp, dc in next 4 sts, (dc, ch 2, dc) in ch-2 sp, dc in next 3 sts, 2 dc in last st. End Color D. (18 sts, 2 ch sp)

ROW 5: Join Color A in first st of previous row, ch 3 (counts as 1 dc), dc in same place, skip 1 st, (dc, ch 1, dc) in next st, ch 1, skip 1 st, (dc, ch 1, dc) in next st, skip 1 st, (2 dc, ch 2, 2 dc) in ch-2 sp, skip 1 st, (dc, ch 1, dc) in next st, ch 1, skip 2 sts, (dc, ch 1, dc) in next st, skip 1 st, (2 dc, ch 2, 2 dc) in ch-2 sp, skip 1 st, (dc, ch 1, dc) in next st, ch 1, skip 1 st, (dc, ch 1, dc) in next st, skip 1 st, 2 dc in last st. End Color A. (24 sts, 10 ch sp)

ROW 6: Join Color B in first st of previous row, ch 3 (counts as 1 dc), dc in same place, skip 1 st, * dc in gap before next st, 2 dc in ch-1 sp, dc in next ch-1 sp, 2 dc in next ch-1 sp, dc in gap before next st **, skip 2 sts, (3 dc, ch 2, 3 dc) in ch-2 sp, skip 2 sts; rep from * once more, then from * to ** once again, skip 1 st, 2 dc in last st. End Color B. (37 sts, 2 ch sp)

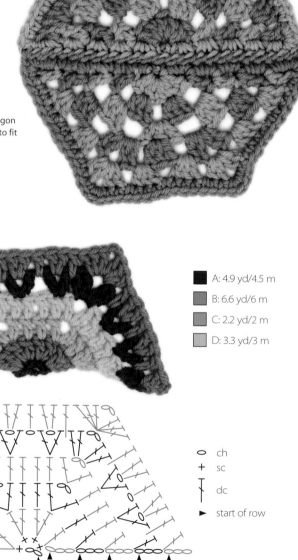

You can also use the half hexagon motif from Mirror on page 28 to fit with 7 in. (18 cm) hexagons.

A: 4.9 yd/4.5 m
B: 6.6 yd/6 m
C: 2.2 yd/2 m
D: 3.3 yd/3 m

○ ch
+ sc
↑ dc
► start of row

5 in. (13 cm)

OPTION 1

FOUNDATION ROW: With Color A, ch 4 (counts as 1 foundation ch, 1 dc).

ROW 1: 6 dc into foundation ch. End Color A. (7 sts)

ROW 2: Join Color B in top of first st of previous row, ch 3 (counts as 1 dc), dc in same place, [2 dc in next st, 3 dc in next st] twice, 2 dc in next 2 sts. End Color B. (16 sts)

ROW 3: Join Color C in first st of previous row, ch 3 (counts as 1 dc), [dc in next 4 sts, 3 dc in next st] twice, dc in next 5 sts. End Color C. (20 sts)

ROW 4: Join Color D in first st of previous row, ch 3 (counts as 1 dc), dc in same place, dc in next 5 sts, (2 dc, 1 tr, 2 dc) in next st, dc in next 6 sts, (2 dc, 1 tr, 2 dc) in next st, dc in next 5 sts, 2 dc in last st. End Color D. (30 sts)

OPTION 2

FOUNDATION ROW: With Color A, ch 4 (counts as 1 foundation ch, 1 dc).

ROW 1: 6 dc into foundation ch. End Color A. (7 sts)

ROW 2: Join Color B in top of first st of previous row, ch 3 (counts as 1 dc), dc in same place, [2 dc in next st] twice, dc in next st, [2 dc in next st] 3 times. End Color B. (13 sts)

ROW 3: Join Color A in first st of previous row, ch 1 and sc in same place, [ch 2, skip 1 st, sc in next st] 6 times. End Color A. (7 sts, 6 ch sp)

ROW 4: Join Color C in first st of previous row, ch 3 (counts as 1 dc), [3 dc in next ch-2 sp] 3 times, ch 1, [3 dc in next ch-2 sp] 3 times, dc in last st. End Color C. (20 sts, 1 ch sp)

ROW 5: Join Color D in first st of previous row, ch 3 (counts as 1 dc), dc in same place, dc in next 6 sts, (2 dc, 1 tr, 2 dc) in next st, dc in next 2 sts, dc in ch-1 sp, dc in next 2 sts, (2 dc, 1 tr, 2 dc) in next st, dc in next 6 sts, 2 dc in last st. End Color D. (31 sts)

ADAPTING HEXAGONS INTO HALF HEXAGONS

Place a ruler across the center of the hexagon chart, just below the corner stitches. Work the pattern, starting at the right-hand edge of the first "half round." Work the pattern in rows, starting each row at the right-hand edge in the first stitch of the previous row, so that all stitches are worked with the right side of the crochet facing you. If there are chain spaces in the corners of the hexagon chart, replace these at the bisected corners with two stitches (the same stitches as used in the rest of the round). Refer to the sample charts provided here for guidance on creating a half hexagon design. The half hexagon below (option 2) is an adaptation of the hexagon used to make the Baby Blanket project (see page 46).

OPTION 1

⬜	A: 1.1 yd/1 m
⬜	B: 2.7 yd/2.5 m
⬜	C: 2.7 yd/2.5 m
⬛	D: 3.8 yd/3.5 m

OPTION 2

⬜	A: 2.2 yd/2 m
⬜	B: 1.6 yd/1.5 m
⬜	C: 2.7 yd/2.5 m
⬛	D: 4.4 yd/4 m

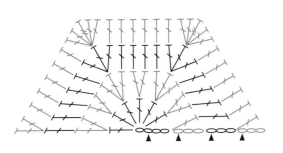

○ ch

Ⅰ dc

ⱦ tr

▶ start of row

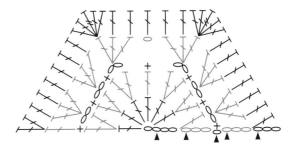

Design Your Own Project

All of the hexagons in this book can be mixed and matched to create a huge array of possible combinations. You could crochet a project using all of the 5 in. (13 cm) hexagons, or using all of the 7 in. (18 cm) hexagons. The choices are endless, so whether you are making a pillow cover or a bedspread, the following guidelines will help you design your own unique item.

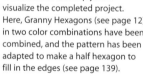

Planning your design

First, decide what you are making and who it is for. This will affect your choice of yarns and colors. For instance, if you are making a baby throw for a girl, perhaps you will choose pink as your main color, and a machine-washable yarn. Or, if you're making a throw for yourself, pick colors and yarns that you love.

CHOOSING HEXAGONS

Choose hexagons that are appropriate for your skill level and that you are comfortable making. You can mix and match as many hexagons as you like, but if you are a beginner, it might be better to choose just one or a few of your favorite hexagons.

CHOOSING YARNS

Pick yarns that are suitable for the finished item. For instance, a baby blanket may be worked in DK, light worsted, or sport-weight yarn. Or a pillow cover could be worked in a smooth, silky yarn. Think about the feel and drape of the finished item and whether the yarn needs to be machine-washable.

CHOOSING COLORS

If you're making a throw for your favorite armchair, choose colors that will match the decor of the room if you want the throw to blend in, or go for contrasting colors if you'd like the throw to be a feature. If you're making a baby blanket, decide whether you'd like soft, pastel colors or bright, cheery colors. You can also make a striking throw by using up scraps in a variety of colors, and edging each hexagon in a neutral color such as cream, white, or black. See opposite for advice on creating a color palette.

DRAWING YOUR DESIGN

Use graph paper or a program on your computer to design your layout. Color the layout using the palette you've chosen to see if it works well. Leave space to add notes on yarn requirements.

JOINING METHOD

Decide which joining method you'd like to use (see page 136). Do you want the joins to be visible and part of the design, or would you rather they were hidden?

CALCULATING YARN QUANTITIES

Each hexagon in this book provides the length of each yarn color required to complete one hexagon. You can use this information to calculate how much yarn you will need for a project, but it is better to make test hexagons for this purpose (see page 135 for more information). If you're not sure you'll have enough yarn, it's preferable to buy an extra skein just in case.

TEST SWATCH

Once you have settled on your design, make a test swatch of four or more hexagons. This is a great way to double-check that your yarn, color, and hexagon choices work well together, and it's also a great way to trial blocking, joining, and washing methods. Block each hexagon and join them with your chosen method. This mini-project will give you a tangible idea of how the actual finished project will look and feel.

A test swatch will help you to visualize the completed project. Here, Granny Hexagons (see page 12) in two color combinations have been combined, and the pattern has been adapted to make a half hexagon to fill in the edges (see page 139).

THE IMPORTANCE OF BLOCKING

When you've made all of the hexagons required, take the time to block them. It really does help to set the stitches and make neat edges for joining and edging. See page 136 for more advice about blocking.

Creating a color palette

Colors are the most important element of your project , but how do you pick the right palette? There is no golden rule or big secret to picking a perfect palette for your project. There are no "wrong" colors. Color triggers an emotional response, and color choice will be different for each person. Combinations that we are drawn to will be unique. Bold, bright colors can be invigorating, while cool, light colors can be calming.

Before setting foot in the yarn store with the intention to buy, spend some time working out the color combinations you are drawn to (see below for some inspiration). Once you have a collection of yarns to work with, try adding new colors and taking colors away. Fiddle about for as long as necessary to get a selection you are happy with. The best course of action is to make test swatches of different combinations before you buy enough yarn for a whole project.

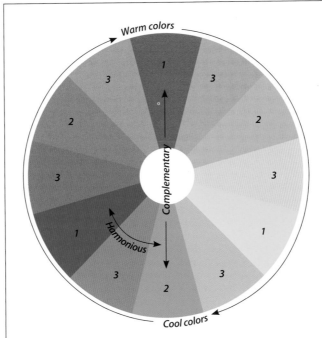

COLOR WHEEL

You can use an artist's color wheel to help you choose colors that go together. The color wheel is made of three primary colors (1): red, blue, and yellow. These are mixed in pairs to create the secondary colors (2): purple, green, and orange. These in turn are mixed with their neighbors to create tertiary colors (3). Opposite colors on the wheel (such as green and red) are "complementary" colors. Adjacent colors on the wheel are harmonious—for example, blue, turquoise, and green.

COOL COLLECTION
Cool colors take up one half of the color wheel. A combination of cool shades will be calming and refreshing. Try adding a touch of cream, black, gray, or white to brighten up the palette. Or, for a really eye-popping palette, add an accent of bright orange.

WARM GLOW
Warm colors take up the other half of the color wheel. Combinations of warm, earthy, fall colors are perfect for a cozy fireside throw. Add a few cool colors or cream to lighten the palette.

PRETTY PASTELS
Pale, pastel colors are suitable for baby items or spring and summer throws. Combinations of pastel colors look fresh and airy. Try adding a touch of a bright color to a pastel palette for contrast.

FUN WITH BRIGHTS
Bright, vivid, and fluorescent colors are eye catching and fun to use in crochet projects. Using a neutral color like black or white to edge granny hexgons made in bright colors helps to unite the colors.

MAKING A STATEMENT
Although black and white are not true colors, when used together they are bold and striking. Add gray and a bold statement color, such as red or electric blue, for a stunning afghan.

PERSONAL PALETTE
Begin with your favorite color (here, green). Add one or two shades of that color. Then look at the color wheel and choose a complementary color (pink). Think about adding a splash of white or black for extra zing. Then add a color two wedges away in either direction from your favorite color on the color wheel (such as blue).

Index

Credits

For my Dad. One less toe but none the worse for wear!

I'd like to give a huge thank you to Quarto for their patience and support throughout this book. I got there in the end—phew! Particular thanks goes to Kate Kirby for understanding and Michelle Pickering for being a rock in a storm of creative chaos.

Thanks as always to Sean, who has suffered the design process with grace and without whom I'd surely starve. Twenty years—time flies!

I'd also like to thank Veronica Holley, Megan Cruden, and Gaye Guerin for being my crafty friends and sources of inspiration.

Last but not least, Ubuntu.

All photographs and illustrations are the copyright of Quarto Publishing plc. While every effort has been made to credit contributors, Quarto would like to apologize should there have been any omissions or errors—and would be pleased to make the appropriate correction for future editions of the book.

With special thanks to Cascade Yarns for providing the yarns used in this book. All yarns are from the Cascade 220 range and are detailed on page 144. www.cascadeyarns.com

Cascade Yarns List

All yarns are from the DK-weight Cascade 220 Superwash range unless indicated otherwise. Every effort has been made to list the correct color number, but please use the following list as a guide only and be sure to check exact colors with your yarn supplier before purchasing.

KEY

Page number / name of hexagon / Cascade 220 range (where relevant) / color code in book / Cascade color number

pp. 12–13 Granny Hexagon A 893, B 822, C 821, D 886, E 823; **Variation** A 821, B 886, C 893, D 875, E 822

pp. 14–15 Lollipop A 914a, B 871; **Variation 1** A 804, B 871; **Variation 2** A 1997, B 871

pp. 16–17 Salacia A 810, B 890, C 887, D 849; **Variation** A 887, B 849, C 810, D 824, E 1997, F 812

pp. 18–19 Fluro 5 in. (13 cm) A 850, B 914a, C 846; **Variation** A 842, B 850, C 812; **7 in. (18 cm)** A 842, B 812, C 850, D 914a, E 846; **Variation** A 914a, B 846, C 812, D 850, E 842

pp. 20–21 Tiles A 1940, B 834, C 839, D 842, E 844, F 883; **Variation** A 883, B 844, C 842, D 1940, E 834, F 839

pp. 22–23 Bracken A 1926, B 841, C 872; **Variation** A 1975, B 1926, C 872

pp. 24–25 Lace Layers A 894, B 903; **Variation** A 847, B 883

pp. 26–27 Lattice Wheel A 851, B 892; **Variation** A 1952, B 892

pp. 28–29 Mirror A 914a, B 1973; **Variation** A 1967, B 1997

pp. 30–31 Fiesta A 823, B 822, C 887, D 807, E 901, F 897, G 844, H 1971; **Variation** A 901, B 823, C 844, D 897, E 1971, F 887, G 807, H 822

p. 32 Marrakesh A 822, B 875, C 807, D 1942, E 886, F 1973

p. 33 Zahra A 908

p. 34 Runde A 871, B 808, C 847, D 810, E 1971

p. 35 Alesund A 847, B 808, C 810, D 1971

p. 36 Spring Stripes A 841, B 850, C 827, D 1941, E 823, F 1942

p. 37 Springtime A 1942, B 841, C 827, D 850, E 1941, F 823

p. 38 Windmill A 887, B 1997, C 810

p. 39 Wheel A 842, B 844, C 849, D 810, E 1997, F 906

p. 40 Spectrum A 809, B 903, C 840, D 824, E 1973, F 812, G 814

p. 41 Pastel Bands A 1973, B 903, C 840, D 812

p. 42 Europa A 822, B 826, C 824, D 851, E 1967, F 1971, G 1973

p. 43 Redshift A 851, B 1967, C 1971, D 822

p. 44 Lace Flower A 887, B 804, C 1986, D 1971

p. 45 Radar A 887, B 804, C 1986, D 1971

pp. 46–47 Baby Blanket project A 834, B 817, C 903, D 1967, E 1942, F 824, G 850

pp. 48–49 Shawl project (Cascade 220 Fingering) A 7824, B 9591, C 7822, D 8012, E 8903, F 7815, G 8910, H 9332

pp. 50–51 Sunshine A 1915, B 820, C 822, D 885, E 846, F 1951; **Variation** A 822, B 820, C 1915, D 846, E 1951, F 885

pp. 52–53 Paper Flower A 894, B 838, C 839, D 886, E 841; **Variation** A 857, B 842, C 840, D 841, E 886

pp. 54–55 Frosty Candy A 894, B 910a, C 901, D 875; **Variation 1** A 840, B 910a, C 1967, D 875; **Variation 2** A 1942, B 910a, C 1973, D 875

pp. 56–57 Dansk A 834, B 910a, C 1921, D 885, E 1951; **Variation** A 897, B 910a, C 885, D 1951, E 1921

pp. 58–59 Arabesque A 1915, B 1975, C 875, D 1942, E 1985; **Variation** A 871, B 879, C 1942, D 875, E 1985

pp. 60–61 Puff Flower A 840, B 850, C 914a, D 871; **Variation 1** A 850, B 914a, C 820, D 871; **Variation 2** A 820, B 840, C 1973, D 871

pp. 62–63 Folk Flower A 848, B 817, C 887, D 820, E 901; **Variation** A 901, B 817, C 848, D 820, E 808

pp. 64–65 Pop Flower A 821, B 834, C 847; **Variation 1** A 821, B 1997, C 847; **Variation 2** A 821, B 842, C 847

pp. 66–67 Cherry Blossom A 816, B 1946, C 910a, D 1921; **Variation** A 1915, B 1940, C 1921, D 1946

pp. 68–69 Ipomoea A 1940, B 844, C 1971; **Variation** A 1941, B 1940, C 884

p. 70 Blume A 850, B 820, C 834, D 1967, E 817, F 840

p. 71 Flor Bonita A 850, B 820, C 834, D 1967, E 840, F 817

p. 72 Skeleton Flower A 827, B 850, C 1941, D 841

p. 73 Seedhead Skeleton A 850, B 827, C 826, D 841

p. 74 Cluster of Grannies A 875, B 834, C 879, D 910a, E 1942, F 1960

p. 75 Grandma's Motif A 910a, B 834, C 1942, D 1960

p. 76 Seashore A 821, B 883, C 896, D 847

p. 77 Starfish A 821, B 847, C 883, D 896

p. 78 Tessellate A 903, B 807, C 908

p. 79 Diamond Flower A 903, B 807, C 908, D 802

p. 80 Popcorn Corners A 1952, B 1975, C 887, D 821, E 906

p. 81 Cluster Corners A 821, B 887, C 906, D 883, E 884

p. 82 Bold Hexagon A 1967, B 910a, 1973, D 1951

p. 83 Bobble Hex A 1951, B 1973, C 910a, D 1967, E 834, F 897

pp. 84–85 Mix-and-Match Blanket project A 910a, B 914a, C 826, D 851, E 1973, F 807, G 1967, H 874

pp. 86–87 Citrus Pillows project (Cascade 220) **Lemon** A 8505, B 7828, C 9076; **Lime** A 8505, B 8910, C 8903; **Orange** A 8505, B 7825, C 9076

pp. 88–89 Hanakotoba A 817, B 1921, C 892, D 900; **Variation** A 817, B 849, C 892, D 900

pp. 90–91 Chocolate Strawberries A 901, B 879, C 819, D 1915, E 818; **Variation** A 818, B 819, C 879, D 901, E 1915

pp. 92–93 Auricula 5 in. (13 cm) A 821, B 807, C 804, D 885; **Variation** A 821, B 893, C 879, D 881; **7 in. (18 cm)** A 839, B 807, C 804, D 821, E 885, F 879, G 893

pp. 94–95 Frilly Flower A 871, B 808, C 851, D 897; **Variation** A 820, B 851, C 871, D 808

pp. 96–97 Starlight A 871, B 896, C 813; **Variation** A 1973, B 813, C 844

pp. 98–99 Checkers A 821, B 886, C 1960, D 1985, E 840, F 881; **Variation** A 821, B 886, C 1960, D 1985, E 840, F 881

pp. 100–101 Ridges A 1942, B 871, C 873, D 819; **Variation** A 824, B 873, C 871, D 1940

pp. 102–103 Irish Rose A 901, B 824, C 1952, D 1986; **Variation** A 824, B 851, C 901, D 812

pp. 104–105 Interlocking A 1915, B 1940, C 827, D 903; **Variation** A 842, B 804, C 807, D 827

pp. 106–107 Candy Swirl Flower A 871, B 808, C 901; **Variation** A 871, B 901, C 1997

p. 108 Little Mill A 839, B 1997, C 810, D 885, E 844

p. 109 Felin Fach A 890, B 817, C 810, D 1973, E 839, F 885, G 875, H 844

p. 110 Ridged Spikes A 851, B 1941, C 827, D 1973, E 849

p. 111 Smooth Spikes A 851, B 834, C 1973

p. 112 Flower Hex A 807, B 1967, C 1915, D 1973

p. 113 Ribbed Hex A 1915, B 1997, C 1973, D 1967, E 839

p. 114 Sirius A 874, B 822, C 826, D 824, E 851

p. 115 Marigold A 874, B 851, C 820, D 826, E 822

p. 116 Rosa Canina A 873, B 910a, C 823, D 855, E 890

p. 117 Pax Romana A 823, B 855, C 910a, D 873, E 890

p. 118 Triangles A 874, B 908, C 891, D 857

p. 119 Wild Rose A 891, B 875, C 908

pp. 120–121 Flower Bag project (Cascade 220) A 7805, B 9422, C 8914, D 8408

pp. 138–139 Half Hexagons 7 in. (18 cm) A 885, B 810, C 887, D 821; **5 in. (13 cm)** A 821, B 887, C 810, D 885